LUCENT LIBRARY OF
BLACK HISTORY

AFRICAN AMERICANS
IN SPORTS

Groundbreakers and Game Changers

By Tamra B. Orr

Portions of this book originally appeared in
African Americans in Sports by Carla Mooney.

LUCENT
PRESS

Published in 2020 by
Lucent Press, an Imprint of Greenhaven Publishing, LLC
353 3rd Avenue
Suite 255
New York, NY 10010

Designer: Deanna Paternostro
Editor: Diane Bailey

Cataloging-in-Publication Data

Names: Orr, Tamra B.
Title: African Americans in sports: groundbreakers and game changers / Tamra B. Orr.
Description: New York : Lucent Press, 2020. | Series: Lucent library of black history | Includes index.
Identifiers: ISBN 9781534568464 (pbk.) | ISBN 9781534568471 (library bound) | ISBN 9781534568488
(ebook)
Subjects: LCSH: African American athletes–History–Juvenile literature. | Racism in sports–United States-
-Juvenile literature. | Discrimination in sports–United States–History–Juvenile literature.
Classification: LCC GV583.O73 2020 | DDC 796.092'396073–dc23

Printed in China

Some of the images in this book illustrate individuals who are models. The depictions do not imply
actual situations or events.

CPSIA compliance information: Batch #BW20KL: For further information contact Greenhaven Publishing LLC, New York, New York at 1-844-317-7404.

Please visit our website, www.greenhavenpublishing.com. For a free color catalog of all our
high-quality books, call toll free 1-844-317-7404 or fax 1-844-317-7405.

CONTENTS

FOREWORD

From medicine and law to sports and literature, African Americans have played a major role in the history of the United States. However, these groundbreaking men and women often faced prejudice and persecution. More than 300 years ago, Africans were taken in chains from their home and enslaved to work for the earliest American settlers. They suffered for more than two centuries under the brutal oppression of their owners until the outbreak of the American Civil War in 1861. After the dust settled four years later and thousands of Americans—both black and white—had died in combat, slavery in the United States had been legally abolished. By the turn of the 20th century, with the help of the 13th, 14th, and 15th Amendments to the U.S. Constitution, African American men had finally won significant battles for the basic rights of citizenship, but the fight for equality was far from over. Even after the successes of the civil rights movement, the struggle continued—and it still continues today.

Although the history of the African American experience is not always a pleasant story, it is also filled with powerful moments of positive change. These triumphs of human equality were achieved with help from brave social activists such as Frederick Douglass, Martin Luther King Jr., and Maya Angelou. They all experienced racial prejudice in their lifetimes and fought by writing, speaking, and acting against it. By exposing the suffering of the black community, they brought people together to try to remedy centuries' worth of wrongdoing.

Today, it is important to learn about the history of African Americans and their experiences in modern America in order to work toward healing the divide that still exists in the United States. This series aims to give readers a deeper appreciation for and understanding of a part of the American story that is often left untold.

Even before the legal emancipation of slaves, black culture was thriving despite many attempts to suppress it. From music to language to art, slaves began cultivating an identity that was completely unique. Soon after these slaves were granted citizenship, African American culture burst into the mainstream. New generations of authors, scholars, painters, and singers were born, and they spread an appreciation for black culture across America and the entire world. Studying the contributions of these talented individuals fosters a sense of optimism. Despite the cruel treatment and racist attitudes these men and women faced, they never gave up, and they helped change the world with their determination and unique voices.

The Lucent Library of Black History offers a glimpse into the lives and accomplishments of some of the most important and influential African Americans across historical time periods and areas of interest. From the arts and sports to the military and politics, the wide variety of topics allows readers to get a full and clear picture of the successes and struggles African Americans have experienced and are continuing to experience. Titles examine primary source documents and quotes from historical and modern figures to provide an enriching learning experience for readers. With detailed timelines, unique sidebars, and a carefully selected bibliography for further research, this series gives readers the tools to independently discover historical events and figures that do not often get their time in the spotlight.

By balancing the harsh realities of the past and present with a sense of hopefulness for the future, the Lucent Library of Black History helps young people understand an essential truth: Black history is a vital part of American history.

SETTING THE SCENE:

1947
Jackie Robinson breaks baseball's color line playing for the Brooklyn Dodgers.

1884
Moses Fleetwood Walker becomes the first black man to play in a Major League Baseball game.

| 1884 | 1936 | 1947 | 1956 | 1967 |

1967
Charlie Sifford becomes the first African American to win a PGA Tour event.

1956
Althea Gibson becomes the first African American tennis player to win a Grand Slam trophy.

1936
Jesse Owens wins four gold medals at the 1936 Olympic Games in Berlin.

A TIMELINE

1968
Tommie Smith and John Carlos silently protest racial injustice after winning medals in the Mexico City Olympics.

2018
Simone Biles becomes the first female gymnast to win four all-around world titles.

2007
Tony Dungy, head coach of the Indianapolis Colts, leads his team to win Super Bowl XLI.

1968   1975   2007   2017   2018

2017
Serena Williams beats her sister Venus in the Australian Open final.

1975
Arthur Ashe is the first black player to be named the top tennis player in the world.

INTRODUCTION

AFRICAN AMERICAN CHAMPIONS

In August 2016, when 19-year-old Simone Biles stepped onto the mat during the Women's Olympic Individual All-Around competition, the audience seemed to sense that a memorable performance was coming. Over the next few minutes, Biles's reputation as one of the most powerful and talented gymnasts in the world proved true. Although this young woman was great at every gymnastic event, she dominated the floor routine. She was amazingly strong, and her last flips and turns were as high and forceful as her first—if not more so. That day, she won four gold medals.

A little over two years later, in 2018, she became the first woman to win four all-around world titles at the World Artistic Gymnastics Championships. In 2019, she stated that gymnastics is "hard mentally and physically. I remember some of the days I'm like: 'Why am I here? What

am I doing? What did I do?' But in the end, it's all worth it, so I'm happy ... Everybody thinks a champion has to always be the winner, come out on top. But I think everybody inside is a champion themselves depending on how you handle your failures and your successes."[1]

Biles's performances came just a few years after another African American gymnast, Gabby Douglas, impressed audiences at several international events. Her amazing releases on the uneven bars earned her the nickname "Flying Squirrel." In 2012, Douglas helped lay the foundation for Biles's success when she became the first African American to take home the gold medal in the Individual All-Around competition at the Olympics.

Over the last century, there have been countless black trailblazers who have broken through racial barriers in sports, but just a few generations ago,

Simone Biles skillfully controlled her movements, her routine, and her audience, keeping them amazed for her entire performance.

it might have been difficult for many people to imagine that the sports world would embrace such astounding African American athletes as Biles and Douglas.

The world has changed a great deal since the late 19th and early 20th centuries. Back then, African American athletes had few opportunities to play. In keeping with the country's trend of segregation, they were banned from most professional sports. According to African American tennis star Arthur Ashe, who rose to fame in the 1960s,

In 1888 major-league baseball barred blacks from their teams. Black cyclists were literally run out of the velodromes [bike-racing arenas]. College football teams had quotas for blacks. Black tennis players were not accepted on the grass courts of Newport, R.I.

The 1920s have been called the Golden Decade of Sports because of the prevalence of such stars as Babe Ruth, Red Grange, Jack Dempsey, Bobby Jones and Bill Tilden. It would be more appropriate to call it the Golden Decade of White Sports, because black athletes were shut out.[2]

Instead of sitting on the sidelines, however, black athletes responded by forming their own clubs, teams, leagues, and tournaments. The Negro National League rose to prominence in baseball, and talented ballplayers impressed and entertained thousands of fans. The United Golf Association encouraged African Americans to come onto the greens. In addition, two of the greatest basketball teams in history, the New York Renaissance and the Harlem Globetrotters, arose during the sporting world's segregation.

Baseball player Jackie Robinson is known for breaking the color barrier in baseball. Many remember this accomplishment as one of the most defining moments for African Americans in professional sports. However, lesser-known athletes in a variety of sports also acted as pioneers for their race. Men and women like tennis star Althea Gibson, golfer Charlie Sifford, and track and field great Jesse Owens had to be faster, stronger, and more skilled to distinguish themselves in a field of white athletes. At the same time, they bore the burden of acting as ambassadors for their race to society at large.

As they pursued excellence, African American athletes often endured discrimination, insults, and sometimes physical violence. Yet persistence and determination drove these men and women to be the best they could. "The black athlete has encountered the ills of a sick society for so long that their determination is far greater than any white athlete,"[3] said Mal Whitfield, a track and field Olympian. For the African American community, black athletes' performances symbolized the hope that they were good enough to share in full citizenship and receive equal treatment.

Over the years, sports have played a major role in how America's white population has come to view and accept African Americans. Some African American athletes, such as basketball great Bill Russell, world heavyweight champion Muhammad Ali, and football star Colin Kaepernick, recognized the unique opportunity that came with their athletic accomplishments. Although their political stances are not always popular with

Colin Kaepernick (center) began kneeling before National Football League (NFL) games as a form of protest.

mainstream America, these athletes used their prominent position in sports as a stage where they could call for equality and highlight the injustice of prejudice. Without the trailblazing men and women of the past, the opportunities for today's African American athletes would not exist. Their sacrifices laid the foundation on which today's superstar black athletes stand.

CHAPTER ONE

ENSLAVEMENT, ENTERTAINMENT, AND ESCAPE

Running, jumping, throwing, and catching have been part of humankind's history for as long as people have lived on the planet. They raced on foot, paddled boats, and swam in rivers and lakes. Most of the time, such activities were not considered games, sports, or competitive activities. Instead, all of this exercise was part of daily life and survival.

Eventually, people did turn physical activities into forms of recreation—and competition—but it took time for the field to be open to everyone. In America, generations passed before black athletes began to join teams—or form their own—and participate in local, state, and national contests. When they did, it could be a form of entertainment or relaxation, but for many, it was also a way to escape poverty.

Sports and Slavery

In the early to mid-19th century, slaves on southern plantations played sports—whether they wanted to or not. According to historian David Wiggins, "It was common for planters to pit individual slaves against each other in wrestling and boxing matches. They frequently took place after corn shucking, log rolling, or other communal gatherings when slaves from all over gathered at one particular plantation. Slaveholders liked nothing better than placing a wager or two on their favorite combatant."[4]

Owners valued slave athletes and took pride in their success. As a reward for winning, slave athletes frequently earned privileges, such as a visit to another plantation or an extra ration of food. Often, slave owners had a deeper motive to encourage their slaves to play sports: It meant that they would not pursue

Slavery was a major focus of the American Civil War, which was fought while Abraham Lincoln was president.

other goals such as learning to read and write, or, even worse, planning a rebellion. As abolitionist and former slave Frederick Douglass wrote, fighting was encouraged because it was "among the most effective means in the hands of the slaveholder in keeping down the spirit of insurrection."[5]

In 1861, the northern and southern states were arguing about the future of slavery in the country. Those in the North thought it should be abolished. The South vehemently disagreed. The hostilities eventually erupted on April 12 when soldiers fired shots at Fort Sumter in South Carolina, beginning the American Civil War. Over the next four years, the North and South battled in a bloody, bitter war. In the end, the North won, and soon after, the states ratified the Thirteenth Amendment to the U.S. Constitution, formally abolishing slavery throughout the United States. Slaves rejoiced, hoping their long-awaited freedom was at hand.

After the initial excitement, the reality of freedom became clear. Approximately 4 million slaves were now free, but most were also poor, illiterate, and homeless. They had few skills to live independently. To survive, many took jobs like those they had done on the plantations, working as sharecroppers, caterers, butchers, barbers, and deliverymen. Those who had excelled at sports also used their talents as a way to make a living and escape poverty.

Opportunities in Horse Racing

In the 1800s, horse racing was popular, so the demand for workers to race, train, and care for horses grew. After the American Civil War ended, horse racing exploded in popularity. Horses were no longer needed on the battlefields, so they could be used in other ways. Towns everywhere built racetracks. Caring for horses was a labor-intensive job that many white people did not want, however. For years, black workers and slaves had tended horses on farms and plantations. Owners realized that these former slaves would give them the best chance of winning races, so they hired them as trainers, groomers, and jockeys. As black jockeys and trainers discovered that their skills with horses were badly needed, it gave them an avenue to improve their lives.

In 1875, the first Kentucky Derby was held in Louisville, Kentucky. On race day, an article in the *Louisville Courier-Journal* predicted, "Today will be history for Kentucky annals as the first 'Derby Day' of what promises

Knowing how to handle and care for horses became one of African Americans' most marketable skills.

to be a long series of annual festivities, which we confidently expect our grandchildren a hundred years hence to celebrate in glorious centennial rejoicings."[6] That first Kentucky Derby made history for African Americans as well, when black jockey Oliver Lewis rode a horse named Aristides to victory. In fact, 13 of the 15 jockeys in the first Derby were black. In the first 28 years of the Kentucky Derby, black jockeys won 15 more times.

An Outstanding Jockey

One of the most famous black Derby winners was a jockey named Isaac Murphy. Born in 1861, Murphy was the son of free black parents. After his father died fighting for the North in the Civil War, Murphy and his mother moved to Lexington, Kentucky. As a boy, Murphy often came with his mother to her job at a racing stable. At the stables, a trainer took note of Murphy's small size and began training him as a jockey. Five days after the first Kentucky Derby, the 14-year-old Murphy made his racing debut. A few months later, Murphy won his first race. By the end of 1876, Murphy had won 11 races. In 1877, he won 19 races and rode in his first Kentucky Derby. A few years later, in 1884, Murphy rode to his first Derby victory. In 1884, Murphy also won the American Derby in Chicago, the most prestigious race of the time. He went on to win this race three more times in 1885, 1886, and 1888.

Murphy's exceptional talent made him one of the most desirable jockeys in racing, and owners clamored for him to ride their horses. Murphy won the Kentucky Derby again in 1890 and 1891, becoming the first jockey to win the event three times.

Murphy's remarkable success in the Kentucky Derby and other prominent national races led many to call him the greatest black athlete of the 19th century. In addition, Murphy rode to victory in a remarkable 34 percent of his races, a feat that is still admired today. In 2018, a memorial honoring him was installed at the Agricultural Science Center at the University of Kentucky. Along with his picture and biographical information is an excerpt from the poem "Praise Song," featured in African American poet Frank X Walker's book *Isaac Murphy: I Dedicate this Ride*. In part, it reads:

*Isaac Murphy's life teach us
how to honor our parents,
how to love full speed,
how to outrun prejudice
         and oppression ...*

*Wrap your arms around
         his story,
close your eyes,
feel the wind whispering in
         your ears.*

*Grab the reins of any
         and everything
that makes your heart race.
Find your purpose. Find
         your purpose.
And hold on.*[7]

This picture of Isaac Murphy was taken in 1895 and shows his riding uniform.

Widespread Discrimination

Despite the success of a handful of black jockeys, the larger black community struggled to survive in the South. After the war, slaves were free but still faced intense discrimination by many white people. Everyday freedoms, such as those involving where black people could live and work or whom they could marry, were severely restricted when Southern states began passing "black code" laws in 1865. The Civil Rights Act of 1866 tried to overrule the black codes, but police departments, courts, and legislatures in the South were controlled by whites, and they routinely intimidated blacks if they tried to assert their legal rights. Too often, if a former slave brought a complaint to the court, the case was simply ignored.

Violence against blacks also increased. White mobs beat blacks and destroyed their property in retaliation for minor offenses. Kidnappings, murders, and lynchings were common. During this time, organized groups like the Ku Klux Klan formed. They terrorized blacks to keep them from challenging white power.

After federal troops left the South in 1877, former slaveholding white Southerners returned to power in state and local governments. Almost immediately, they passed laws to segregate the races. These laws were called Jim Crow laws, named after a popular 19th-century minstrel song that stereotyped blacks. While the specifics of Jim Crow laws differed in each state, they shared similar characteristics. They restricted where blacks could live, work, go to school, and worship. They required blacks to use separate public facilities. Like the earlier black codes, Jim Crow laws tried to block blacks from voting by requiring them to take literacy tests that were difficult or impossible to pass or to pay taxes they could not afford.

Some Jim Crow laws forced blacks to act subservient to whites. Blacks had to tip their hats to whites and step out of their way as they passed on the street or sidewalk. In stores, black customers were only served after whites, if at all. Blacks also had to address whites with respectful titles like "sir" and "ma'am," while whites typically referred to adult blacks as "boy" and "girl," or used offensive racial slurs.

By the late 1800s, conditions for blacks were steadily getting worse. Segregation was on the rise, and laws forbidding discrimination in public places were overturned. When

African American men are shown here carrying a coffin down the street to protest Jim Crow segregation laws.

the U.S. Supreme Court ruled in *Plessy v. Ferguson* to uphold "separate but equal" laws in 1896, it became legal for states to have separate facilities for the two races. Throughout many communities, blacks and whites were officially segregated, forced to go to separate—but far from equal—schools, restrooms, theaters, and restaurants.

Leaving the Tracks

This discrimination soon made its way to the racetrack. At first, white riders did not challenge black jockeys. However, as racing got more popular, the money increased, and by the 1880s, riding horses became a way for disadvantaged young men of all races to move upward socially and economically.

As discrimination and segregation increased, bands of white jockeys formed "anti-colored" unions and attempted to force black jockeys off the track. They would gang up on black jockeys during races, ensuring that they did not win. According to a 1900 Chicago newspaper account,

A black boy would be pocketed, thrust back in the race; or his mount would be bumped out of contention; or a white boy would run alongside, slip a foot under a black boy's stirrup and toss him out of the saddle. Again while ostensibly whipping their own horses those white fellows would slash out and cut the nearest Negro rider. They nearly ran the black boys off the tracks.[8]

In 1894, white riders established the Jockey Club, an administrative organization for the horse-racing industry. One of its responsibilities was to license jockeys; only licensed jockeys could ride in organized horse races. However, the club restricted the number of black jockeys it licensed, reducing their numbers in the sport.

Licensed black jockeys also received fewer invitations to ride horses. Owners feared white jockeys would gang up against a black rider on the track, making sure he did not win. Fewer mounts and limited licenses resulted in a dramatic drop in black jockeys in the United States. While a few still managed to have some success in important races, most could no longer make a living at racing. Instead, many black jockeys headed to Europe, where they were welcomed and could make a living. By the 1930s, less than 1 percent of licensed jockeys were black. Even Isaac Murphy, the sport's pioneer African American jockey, was out of racing entirely by the early 1890s.

A Fighting Chance

Another popular sport on prewar southern plantations was boxing. Matches pitted slave against slave, and many wagers were made on who would win. Talented fighters could win a fortune for white owners who bet on a match and won.

FREED TO FIGHT

Tom Molineaux was born a slave in Virginia in 1784. Trained to box by his father, Molineaux fought fellow slaves. After beating a rival plantation's slave, he earned a significant sum for his owner. As a reward, the owner gave Molineaux his freedom and $500.

In 1809, Molineaux sailed to England. He worked with trainer Bill Richmond, another freed American slave who had moved to England and become a prize-fighter. Molineaux's impressive bare-knuckle boxing performances led to a title match against British heavyweight legend Tom Cribb.

In December 1810, when Molineaux and Cribb faced off, most people expected Cribb to win easily. However, Molineaux proved to be a smart and powerful boxer. Cribb did win eventually—but not until the fight had lasted an incredible 39 rounds. According to Des Kilbane, creator of "Crossing the Black Atlantic," a documentary about Molineaux's life, "The crowd decided that [there was] no way their champion [Cribb] was going to lose. In the 19th round, Molineaux had Cribb in a headlock ... The crowd stormed the ring and broke Molineaux's fingers."[1] In 1811, Molineaux and Cribb fought for a second time. This time, Cribb retained his title with an 11th-round knockout.

After the Cribb fights, Molineaux became a celebrity in England and Ireland. He fought other bouts and exhibitions. He died at age 34, but as Kilbane stated in a trailer for the film, "He broke some of the conventions around boxing. He astounded people at the time and it remains a remarkable story."[2]

1. James Wilson, "New Documentary on Ex-Virginia Slave Who Died as a Champion Galway Boxer," Irish Central, September 27, 2017. www.irishcentral.com/roots/history/born-a-virginia-slave-he-died-penniless-in-galway.

2. Des Kilbane, "Crossing the Black Atlantic trailer," YouTube video, 1:53, June 9, 2017. www.youtube.com/watch?v=T0oZyXzAlDw.

After the war, black boxers kept punching to make a living. However, many were limited by racism from whites in the sport. While white boxers would fight blacks on the way to the crown, once they achieved boxing prominence, they refused to face black opponents.

Peter Jackson was one of the most famous 19th-century black boxers. Born in the Virgin Islands, Jackson began his boxing career in

1882 in Australia. In 1886, he won the Australian heavyweight title by knocking out white boxer Tom Leeds. Following his victory, Jackson moved to the United States, where he found that white fighters were reluctant to face him. Instead, he fought another black boxer, George Godfrey, and won the world "colored" heavyweight championship in 1888.

As the new black heavyweight champion, Jackson found white fighters were more willing to fight him. They hoped that by defeating Jackson, they could set up their own title fights for the world heavyweight championship. For his part, Jackson hoped that if he defeated respected white fighters, he might also have a chance to fight for the world title.

In 1890, John L. Sullivan was the world heavyweight champion. Although several athletic clubs made lucrative offers to host a fight between Sullivan and Jackson, Sullivan refused to fight Jackson, called "the Black Prince," because of his color. For years, Jackson unsuccessfully tried to set up a title fight with Sullivan, but Sullivan never agreed. As the defending champion, he stated there were no other fighters who were worth fighting. Jackson died in 1901, never getting the chance to prove in the ring that he was the world's best.

The Worcester Whirlwind

Although Jackson was denied the opportunity to fight for boxing's ultimate prize, other 19th-century black athletes were more fortunate. A young black man named Marshall "Major" Taylor overcame prejudice and discrimination to become the premier bicycle rider of the day.

In the late 1800s, the cycling craze was spreading across America. By 1890, there were more than 100,000 cyclists, and almost every town had cycling clubs for men, women, and children. There were also clubs for blacks. Soon, bicycling became an organized sport. Velodromes, or bike-racing arenas, were constructed across the United States. Fans came to watch cyclists race around the tracks at top speed.

Born in rural Indiana, Major Taylor received his first bicycle from a wealthy white family that employed his father as a coachman. In 1892, a local bike shop in Indianapolis hired him to perform cycling stunts outside the shop. He earned the nickname "Major" because he wore a soldier's uniform as a costume during the performances. Taylor worked in

MAJOR TAYLOR

CYCLISME

Major Taylor is shown here with his bicycle and his racing uniform.

bicycle shops and was guided by Birdie Munger, a former cycling star. Under Munger's tutoring, Taylor was introduced to professional cycling. He won his first race in 1892 at age 13.

In 1894, the League of American Wheelmen, bicycling's governing body, banned blacks from amateur racing against whites. Nonetheless, Taylor proved his talent competing in races against other black cyclists and became the black cycling champion.

When Munger moved to Worcester, Massachusetts, in 1895 to open a bicycle factory, Taylor moved with him. He found Worcester a more welcoming place to train. "I was in Worcester only a very short time before I realized that there was no such race prejudice existing among the bicycle riders there as I had experienced in Indianapolis,"[9] Taylor wrote in his autobiography, *The Fastest Bicycle Rider in the World.*

By 1896, Taylor had broken two world track records for paced and unpaced 1-mile (1.6 km) rides on an Indianapolis track. To punish him for this success, whites banned him from Indianapolis's Capital City track. Taylor's sprinting speed, however, proved he was ready to ride in professional races. A New York racing board that opposed the color ban agreed to register him as a professional.

Taylor faced many challenges because of his race. In 1897, many southern race promoters would not permit him to enter their races. When he was allowed, people along the route tried to sabotage him, shoving sticks in his wheels as he rode past. In addition, white riders often abused and threatened him. In a race in Boston, Massachusetts, a competitor pulled Taylor from his bike and choked him to unconsciousness. In Atlanta, Georgia, he was threatened if he did not leave town within 48 hours. In some cities, hotel managers refused him lodging.

Despite these setbacks, Taylor's feats soon became legendary. By 1898, he held seven world records in his specialty of sprint races. In 1899, Taylor won the world 1-mile championship in Montreal, Canada. The following year, he completed the national championship series and was crowned the American sprint champion.

Eventually, Taylor, like other black athletes, decided to try his luck outside the United States. In 1901, he signed with the European bike tour and beat every European champion. From 1902 to 1904, Taylor competed in races in Europe, Australia, New Zealand, and the United States. He became known as the fastest bicyclist in the world. When Taylor retired in 1910 at age 32, he had won hundreds of races and was an international star.

In 2008, a granite and bluestone monument honoring Taylor was erected at the Worcester Public Library. It invites visitors to learn about the world champion cyclist. "If you're dealing with adversity yourself, trying to get good grades, play sports, then he's an example of an African-American dealing with adversity who was able to overcome all that,"[10] stated Paul Lupica, a teacher and cyclist in Worcester. In 2019, the Worcester courthouse also set up a special display of Taylor. His great-granddaughter Karen Donovan attended the ceremony.

By 1910, automobiles were grabbing the attention of the public. Bicycles began to fade into the background, unable to keep pace as complex motors replaced simple pedals. However, athletes like Taylor are still remembered for both their talents on two wheels and their perseverance in a time of racial divide.

CHAPTER TWO
NEW CENTURY, OLD CONFLICTS

At the start of the 20th century, most of America was starkly split into black and white. This racial division extended to black athletes even when they were clearly superior to whites in the same sport. Forced out of white leagues, they had little choice but to establish their own leagues and teams.

On the Baseball Diamond

Long known as "America's pastime," baseball started becoming popular in the United States in the middle of the 19th century. In 1869, the first professional baseball team formed, the Cincinnati Red Stockings, followed two years later by the first professional league. Between 1865 and 1890, a number of black athletes played on minor league teams made up mostly of whites. While many only played for a brief time because of local prejudice and unofficial color bans, a few black athletes had successful careers in professional baseball.

Moses Fleetwood Walker became the first black athlete to play in major league baseball. In 1883, Walker signed as a catcher with the minor league Toledo Blue Stockings of the Northwestern League. A year later, the Toledo team joined the American Association, which was considered a major league at the time.

Walker played 42 games for Toledo, but even members of his own team discriminated against him. Toledo teammate and pitcher Tony Mullane refused to take signals from him. "[Moses] Walker was the best catcher I ever worked with ... but whenever I had to pitch to him I used to pitch anything I wanted without looking at his signals," said Mullane. "He caught me and caught anything I pitched without knowing what was coming."[11] Walker did not last long in the majors. In July 1884, he broke a rib during a game and was released by Toledo. He spent the next five years playing for other teams and leagues. By the end of the 19th century, baseball salaries were climbing and roster spots became incredibly competitive. It was clear to baseball executives that any position given to a black player meant one that did not go to a white player. Finally, in 1887, the prestigious International League decided that each team could only have one black player. As a result, 1889 was Walker's last season in baseball.

In 2018, a mural of the baseball pioneer was painted in downtown Steubenville, Ohio, and an official Moses Fleetwood Walker Day was established. Rich Donnelly, a former baseball player and coach, stated, "When you are the first in the world to do something, you are really special. [Walker] had enough courage and guts to survive being beat down and yelled at to get to his dream of playing Major League baseball."[12]

Another Way to Play

By the beginning of the 20th century, the color line in Major League Baseball (MLB) was firmly in place, and it would stay that way for almost 50 years. However, the abundant talent among black athletes would not be suppressed.

The first black professional team was the Cuban Giants, a baseball team organized in 1885 in New York. Other teams soon followed. From early spring to late fall, they traveled around the country, challenging local teams in small towns and rural areas. They played black or white teams, on sandlots or in major league stadiums. "We played baseball every day," said Arthur W. Hardy, a pitcher on the Topeka Giants from 1906 to 1912. "We started in Topeka and we played up through Kansas, Iowa, and into Illinois and Chicago. And then we played back in those little country towns."[13] By the end of the 19th century, all-black baseball teams were commonplace.

Between 1900 and 1920, many famous black baseball teams were formed. These included the Chicago American Giants, the New York Lincoln Giants, and the Homestead Grays in Pennsylvania. The rivalries between them were intense. Because independent teams had no league or tournament to formally crown a champion, any team could claim to hold the title of world champion of the black teams. If they did so, they were usually challenged by another team to play for the championship.

While some teams were successful, others lasted only a season or two.

By the end of World War I in 1918, black baseball was popular with urban black populations across the country. In 1920, Andrew "Rube" Foster, the manager of the Chicago American Giants, had grown tired of teams stealing each other's best players, so he proposed a national association for the Negro baseball clubs. He recruited owners of the top midwestern black teams, and together they formed the Negro National League. Initially, it had eight teams. The league held its first game on May 2, 1920, and continued to play throughout the 1920s until it fell apart during the Great Depression of the 1930s.

A second Negro National League, formed in 1933 by wealthy tavern owner Gus Greenlee, followed Foster's league.

The Chicago Union Giants, shown here in 1905, became a Negro National League team.

Soon, this league was the driving force behind black baseball. Other leagues formed during this time, including the Negro Southern League and the Negro American League. Despite the Depression, these leagues prospered. During World War II, they grew to be a $2 million-a-year industry, one of the most successful examples of a black-owned business in the United States.

A Negro League Star

The Negro leagues were home to many legendary baseball players. One of the greatest was Josh Gibson, a right-handed slugger nicknamed the "black Babe Ruth." In the batter's box, Gibson excited crowds. Every time he stepped up to the plate, fans expected his swing to crack a home run, each farther than the last. "It was just a treat to watch him hit the ball. There was no effort at all,"[14] said William Julius "Judy" Johnson, one of Gibson's first managers.

Born in 1911, Gibson started playing baseball as a teenager for a semi-pro team. When he was 18, Gibson attended a Negro league game between the Homestead Grays and the Kansas City Monarchs. When Homestead's catcher, Buck Ewing, injured his hand, Johnson, the team manager, went looking in the stands for Gibson. Johnson later recalled, "I asked him if he wanted to catch and he said 'yes, sir,' so we had to hold up the game while he went and put on Buck Ewing's uniform ... We signed him the next day."[15]

Gibson quickly became a star. Over his 17-year career, he was credited with hitting almost 800 home runs. He won 12 home-run titles and 4 batting crowns. Gibson's home runs were known for being spectacularly deep. He often sent balls flying more than 500 feet (152 m). One homer was reportedly measured at 575 feet (175 m). Some reports say that Gibson hit a fair ball out of New York's Yankee Stadium, the only hitter ever to do so.

Gibson played his entire career in the Negro leagues. He died in 1947, at age 35, and in 1972, he was inducted into the National Baseball Hall of Fame. Nearly 50 years after his death, in 1994, the Josh Gibson Foundation was established. This non-profit matches students from the University of Pittsburgh with elementary and middle school students for tutoring.

Satch's "Pistol Bullet"

Pitcher Leroy "Satchel" Paige dominated Negro league baseball from the late 1920s through the mid-1940s before joining the Cleveland Indians in 1948.

Josh Gibson was one of the most gifted baseball players of his time.

RENAISSANCE MAN

Attending Rutgers College in 1915 on a full academic scholarship, Paul Robeson also excelled in sports. He earned 15 varsity letters in football, baseball, basketball, and track and field. In football, he was twice named a first-team All-American. As the school's first African American football player, he endured discrimination. His locker was segregated from the rest of the team, and when the team traveled, Robeson stayed in black-only hotel rooms. During his freshman year, Robeson was banned from the annual football banquet.

Sometimes Robeson also faced physical injury. In one scrimmage, teammates hit Robeson so hard that he left with a dislocated shoulder and a broken nose. Another time, a player stepped on his hand with such force that his cleats ripped off Robeson's fingernails.

Despite this treatment, Robeson became a spectacular player. After college, he played professional football for a few years and used his salary to pay for law school. He practiced law briefly, but soon turned to acting and singing. Later, he focused on promoting African and African American history and culture in theater and music.

In 2019, an art museum in Somerville, New Jersey, where Robeson attended high school, featured six portraits of the man known by many as "a renaissance man, a social activist, scholar, intellectual, lawyer, All-American athlete, singer, linguist, humanist, and advocate for international peace."[1]

1. Cynthia Medina, "Art Exhibit Captures Many Faces of Paul Robeson, SHS '19," Tap into Somerville, February 7, 2019. www.tapinto.net/towns/somerville/articles/art-exhibit-captures-many-faces-of-paul-robeson-shs-19.

Paul Robeson, shown here in 1925, was a superior all-around athlete.

*Satchel Paige joined the
Cleveland Indians after many
years in the Negro leagues.*

Paige's pitching was legendary, and his showboating—entertaining behavior on the field—earned him legions of fans. Hall of Famer Joe DiMaggio said that Satchel Paige was the best and fastest pitcher he ever faced. Over a four-decade career, Paige recorded feats such as 64 consecutive scoreless innings and a 21-game winning streak. He threw more pitches, usually strikes, for more seasons than any pitcher past or present.

Nicknamed "Satchel" after working as a baggage carrier, Paige joined the Negro Southern League in 1926. Soon everyone was talking about the tall, lanky pitcher. During the off-season, he traveled around the world playing in other countries and on exhibition teams against white major leaguers.

Paige's most famous pitch was the hesitation pitch. When throwing it, he deliberately paused when his left foot hit the ground. Over six exhibition games in 1934 to 1935, Paige beat baseball's best white pitcher of the time, Jay Hanna "Dizzy" Dean. "My fastball looks like a change of pace alongside that pistol bullet old Satch shoots up to the plate," Dean said. "If Satch and I were pitching on the same team, we'd clinch the pennant by the fourth of July and go fishing until World Series time."[16] As a Negro league star, Paige made as much as $40,000 per year, more than any other African American player at the time. Paige was also given a chance in the big leagues when the Cleveland Indians needed a pitcher for the 1948 pennant race. At age 42, he became the first African American pitcher in Major League Baseball—and the oldest rookie in the majors—and helped his team win the pennant.

Paige's longevity was astounding. In 1965, at age 59, Paige threw three scoreless innings for Kansas City. When asked about his age, Paige became famous for saying, "Age is a question of mind over matter. If you don't mind, it doesn't matter."[17]

Jack Johnson Takes the Title

Although most black athletes played in separate leagues during the early 1900s, some successfully participated in predominantly white sports such as boxing. Born in 1878 in Texas, Jack Johnson began boxing as a teenager. At the time, black boxers could compete for some titles, but not for the world heavyweight championship.

For 14 years, Johnson boxed and built his reputation and wealth by winning matches against both black and white fighters. Looking to fight the best in the world, Johnson repeatedly challenged James J. Jeffries, the

A TRAVELING TEAM

While some black athletes wowed crowds at the baseball diamonds, others took their skills indoors to the basketball courts. The all-black New York Renaissance, or "Rens," played teams throughout the United States, winning more than 2,000 games during their 25 years. Because professional basketball leagues would not accept a black team, the Rens barnstormed across the country, showcasing their skills and fancy passes. The Rens played all types of teams—and handily defeated them.

During one stretch from 1932 to 1933, the Rens won an amazing 88 straight games. "To this day, I have never seen a team play better team basketball," said Hall of Fame coach John Wooden, who played against the Rens as a member of the barnstorming Indianapolis Kautskys during the 1930s. "They had great athletes, but they weren't as impressive as their team play. The way they handled and passed the ball was just amazing to me then, and I believe it would be today."[1]

1. Quoted in John Hareas, "Remembering the Rens," NBA, accessed on April 23, 2019. www.nba.com/history/encyclopedia_rens_001214.html.

white heavyweight champion, to a match. However, Jeffries refused to fight Johnson. Instead, he retired undefeated. Johnson's chance at the title came in 1908 when the new heavyweight champion, Tommy Burns, agreed to fight him. At a match in Australia, Johnson beat Burns to become the world's first African American heavyweight champion. According to Johnson biographer Randy Roberts, whites found Johnson's win hard to take. "The press reacted [to Johnson's victory] as if Armageddon [the end of the world] was here."[18]

Out of the boxing ring, Johnson's public image upset many whites. He wore fancy clothes, drove flashy cars, and openly dated and married white women. "Johnson ruptured role after role set aside for Negroes in American society,"[19] said historian Lawrence Levine.

Some refused to acknowledge Johnson as the world heavyweight champion. They arranged fights against white boxers, called "great white hopes," to take back the title, but with no success. Finally, boxing promoters convinced former champion Jeffries to come out of retirement to fight Johnson. Promoted as the "Battle of the Century," the fight took place on July 4, 1910, in Reno, Nevada. After Johnson downed Jeffries in the 15th round, deadly race riots erupted across the country. To prevent more violence, Congress passed an act banning the interstate transport of fight films,

Jack Johnson (right) was eager to face white opponents, such as Canada's Tommy Burns (left). Johnson beat Burns in this 1908 heavyweight championship fight.

fearing that the movies of Johnson winning would cause more violence.

In 1913, Johnson went to Europe following a scandal involving a white woman and a court conviction. In 1920, he returned to the United States to serve his eight-month sentence in federal prison. After his release, he boxed a few more matches but retired in 1928. He died in a car crash in 1946. One of the best fighters ever to step into the ring, Johnson was considered an icon. "Johnson in many ways is an embodiment of the African-American struggle to be truly free in this country—economically, socially and politically," said filmmaker Ken Burns, who chronicled Johnson's story in the 2005 film *Unforgivable Blackness: The Rise and Fall of Jack Johnson.* "He absolutely refused to play by the rules set by the white establishment, or even those of the black community. In that sense, he fought for freedom not just as a black man, but as an individual."[20]

The "Brown Bomber"

Despite Johnson's remarkable career, it was another boxer named Joe Louis who won the hearts of all Americans, black and white. Born in Alabama in 1914, Joseph Louis Barrow began boxing as a young man after moving to Detroit, Michigan. After winning 50 out of 54 amateur bouts, Louis turned pro in 1934. As a professional, he won his first 27 fights, 23 of them by knockout. His undefeated streak ended in 1936 when German boxer Max Schmeling beat him.

After his first professional loss, Louis returned to training with one mission—to face Schmeling in a rematch and defeat him. In the meantime, Louis became the world heavyweight champion in 1937. Louis's powerful performances in the boxing ring made him a hero to the black community. Malcolm X, who became a leader of the militant wing of the civil rights movement, was a boy when Louis took the world championship. He once commented, "Every Negro boy old enough to walk wanted to be the next Brown Bomber."[21]

The following year, it was time for the rematch with Schmeling. At that time, Adolf Hitler and the Nazi Party in Germany were growing powerful. For many Americans, German boxer Schmeling represented Hitler and the fascist Nazi ideology, while Louis stood for America and democracy. Before the bout, Louis was invited to the White House, where President Franklin Roosevelt told him that the United States needed muscles like his to beat Germany.

At New York's Yankee Stadium, Louis knocked Schmeling to the mat three times in front of a crowd of 70,000. Within two minutes, the "Brown Bomber" had knocked out his rival, winning the match. In the process, Louis became an American hero. "What my father did was enable white America to think of him as an American, not as a black," said his son, Joe Louis Jr. "By winning, he became white America's first black hero."[22]

Unlike Johnson, Louis carefully cultivated his image outside the ring. He was never photographed with a white woman, never gloated over beating a white boxer, and never demonstrated emotion in public. He also showed his patriotism by enlisting in the army when the United States entered World War II. He raised money for the war effort and donated part of his winnings to military relief funds. "Joe Louis set a stunning example through his acts of patriotism,"[23] stated historian Jeffrey Sammons.

Louis held the world heavyweight title for almost 12 years, the longest of any boxer, and he retired undefeated in 1949. Upon his death in 1981, at the request of President Ronald Reagan, Louis was buried in Arlington National Cemetery.

On the Track

In the 1930s, black Americans were treated as second-class citizens. When facing the threat of Nazi Germany, however, Americans put aside their differences to unify behind national pride. In 1936, a young black track star named Jesse Owens electrified the country with his record-setting performance at the Olympic Games, where he won four gold medals. The young black man became America's greatest national track hero.

Born the son of an Alabama cotton picker, James Cleveland Owens quickly became a high school track star. Although he set records for the long jump and 100-yard dash, he was not offered a college scholarship. Nevertheless, Owens enrolled at Ohio State University. His fleet-footed performances earned him national recognition. As a sophomore, he soundly defeated the best college athletes at the 1935 Big Ten track and field championships. In a single meet, Owen bested three world records and tied a fourth.

While Owens was smashing track records, Nazism was growing in Germany. The world was on the verge of World War II even as the 1936 Olympics were scheduled to be held in Berlin, Germany. Nazi leader Adolf Hitler believed the Olympics would be

*Owens set a world record in the long jump
at the Berlin Olympics in 1936.*

a world stage for his athletes to demonstrate their superiority. To his dismay, Owens ran and jumped his way to four gold medals in the 100- and 200-meter dashes, the long jump, and the 4 x 100-meter relay. He became the first American track and field athlete to win four gold medals in a single Olympic Games. His performances thrilled the world and unified Americans.

After the Games, Owens returned home to a ticker tape parade in New York City. Despite his spectacular performances, however, Owens encountered discrimination in his own country. For a reception in his honor at New York's Waldorf-Astoria Hotel, Owens was asked to ride the freight elevator. "When I came back to my native country, after all the stories about Hitler, I couldn't ride in the front of the bus," Owens said. "I had to go to the back door. I couldn't live where I wanted. I wasn't invited to shake hands with Hitler, but I wasn't invited to the White House to shake hands with the President, either."[24]

Owens used his fame to travel as an inspirational speaker,

addressing youth groups and professional organizations. He attended sports banquets and many events to share his stories. He also devoted much of his time to working with underprivileged youth, becoming a board member and director of the Chicago Boys' Club.

In February 1979, President Jimmy Carter presented Owens with the Living Legend Award. "A young man who possibly didn't even realize the superb nature of his own capabilities went to the Olympics and performed in a way that I don't believe has ever been equaled since ... and since this superb achievement, he has continued in his own dedicated but modest way to inspire others to reach for greatness,"[25] Carter said about Owens.

As World War II ended in 1945 and the Allies celebrated their victory, more and more people began to call for social and racial justice. African Americans had proven themselves in the most serious of circumstances, showing their bravery, competence, and skills on the battlefield. In addition, they continued to accomplish great feats in sports, where they had demonstrated their talents and prowess on baseball diamonds and basketball courts, in boxing rings and around tracks in the United States and abroad. Finally, it was time to focus on eliminating the color barrier in sports and recognizing African Americans as the champions they were.

CHAPTER THREE
THE POWER OF PROTEST

World War II dramatically changed race relations in some ways. With African Americans serving in all of the armed forces and fighting on the front lines, it was difficult and impractical to keep them separate from their white counterparts, especially in the chaos of battle. Weapons paid no attention to color, wounding blacks and whites without preference. Despite the unity that many blacks and whites shared during the war, and the brave actions of African American soldiers such as the Tuskegee Airmen and an all-black Army Air Corps, the United States continued to discriminate.

For years, the United States had battled for democracy and equal rights in Europe, but at home, Americans still permitted Jim Crow laws to exist. The black community was acutely aware of the country's ongoing hypocrisy—and it was their moment to protest more strongly than ever.

Breaking the Color Line

The *Pittsburgh Courier* was one of the most prominent black newspapers in the 1930s and 1940s, well known for its sports coverage. Sportswriter Wendell Smith was one of the *Courier*'s most influential journalists, using his pen to gain support for Jackie Robinson to become the first black player in modern Major League Baseball in 1947.

As a teenager, Smith had been a ballplayer and experienced the effects of segregation himself. After he pitched a shutout, a game in which the other team does not score, a baseball scout still passed him over and signed the opposing team's pitcher, who was white. The scout told Smith that he wished he could sign him but could not because of his race. "That's when I decided that if I ever got into a position to do anything, I'd dedicate my life to getting Negro players into the big leagues,"[26] Smith later said.

At the *Courier*, Smith launched a campaign to end segregation in organized baseball. He interviewed eight managers and forty players in the National League about integration, and then wrote a series of articles in 1939 titled "What Big Leaguers Think of Negro Baseball Players." In the interviews, only one manager stated that blacks should be banned from organized baseball. The other managers and players said that they would welcome black players if league officials allowed it.

By the end of the 1930s, white attitudes were starting to change, and a groundswell of protest arose over baseball's color line. The *Courier* reported on the increasing criticism of baseball's discrimination. World War II gave Smith even more opportunity to protest the exclusion of black athletes from baseball. As Smith said, "Big league baseball is perpetuating the very things thousands of Americans are overseas fighting to end, namely, racial discrimination and segregation."[27]

Smith kept working to break baseball's color line. He blasted team owners who would not recruit black players and organized a meeting where the black press could argue the case for including blacks in the major leagues.

Nearly a year and a half later, Branch Rickey, president and general manager of the Brooklyn Dodgers, decided that he would secretly scout for black players. In April 1945, he asked Smith if he knew of any black players capable of playing in the majors. Smith responded, "I do know of a player who could make it. His name is Jackie Robinson."[28] Smith wrote in his column, "It appears to me that Branch Rickey, one of the wisest and shrewdest men in baseball, looms as a valuable friend, both for organized Negro baseball and the cause of the Negro player in the majors."[29]

A Ballplayer with Guts

In an interview years later, Smith admitted that he did not think that Robinson was necessarily the best black ballplayer, but he did believe he was the right man to join the white major leagues. In college, Robinson had played on an integrated team. He excelled at several sports and was one of the greatest all-around athletes at the University of California, Los Angeles (UCLA).

Born in 1919, Jack Roosevelt Robinson grew up in a working-class neighborhood in Pasadena,

California. Even as a child, he was a fierce competitor, and this drive continued into college. At UCLA, he became the school's first athlete to letter in four sports—football, basketball, baseball, and track. He also earned a reputation as a fighter, brawling with any white man who insulted him. After college, Robinson served in the army during World War II and then joined the Negro leagues in 1945 as a shortstop for the Kansas City Monarchs.

As Robinson settled into his first season with the Monarchs, Rickey was sending out his scouts, looking for players. The name most often mentioned was Robinson's, but he was unaware that major league scouts were watching him.

The glowing reports convinced Rickey that Robinson was his man. Still, he knew that the first black man to cross baseball's color line would have to endure criticism and insults from fans, competitors, and teammates. He wanted to be sure that Robinson could stand up to the abuse. In August 1945, Rickey met with Robinson in his Brooklyn office. Robinson thought that he was going to be offered a spot with other black players on Rickey's Negro league team, the Brooklyn Brown Dodgers. Instead, Rickey told Robinson that he wanted him to play for the regular Brooklyn team. During the interview Rickey described all the insults Robinson would likely face. Rickey told him, "I want a ballplayer with guts enough not to fight back. You've got to do this job with base hits and stolen bases and fielding ground balls, Jackie. Nothing else."[30] At the end of the meeting, the two agreed that Robinson would play for the minor league Montreal Royals, the Dodgers' top farm team, or training team, in 1946.

An MVP

Professional baseball's color line cracked on April 18, 1946, when Robinson debuted as the Royals' second baseman. That season, he earned a .349 batting average, the best in the minor leagues, stole 40 bases, and led his team to the Little World Series championship. The following year, on April 15, 1947, Robinson was called up to his first major league game for the Brooklyn Dodgers.

At first, the reactions to Robinson were mixed. Almost all blacks applauded his joining the team, and some whites did too. However, other whites, including a number of Major League Baseball players, opposed Robinson playing in the majors. Even some of his own teammates protested having him on the team. Bill Nack of *Sports Illustrated* wrote that "Robinson was the target of racial epithets and flying cleats, of hate letters and death threats, of pitchers throwing at his head and legs, and catchers spitting on his shoes."[31] As some people harassed Robinson, others supported him. In one memorable moment, in the face of hostile fans, teammate Pee Wee Reese walked over to Robinson and put his arm around him. When some of Robinson's teammates threatened to sit out rather than play with him, Dodgers manager Leo Durocher told them that he would trade them before he traded Robinson. Other men, including league president Ford Frick, baseball commissioner Happy Chandler, and Jewish baseball star Hank Greenberg, also defended Robinson's right to play in the major leagues.

Through it all, Robinson handled the pressure of

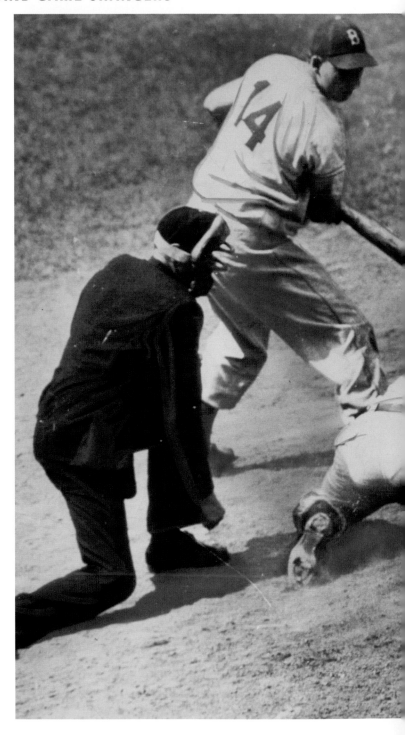

Robinson is shown here sliding into home plate during a game in 1948.

being baseball's trailblazer with dignity. He put aside the prejudice and proved how talented he was. In his first year in the majors, Robinson hit 12 home runs, led the National League in stolen bases, and won Rookie of the Year. His play also helped the Dodgers win the National League pennant. During 1949, Robinson hit an impressive .342 batting average, led the league in stolen bases again, and earned the National League's Most Valuable Player (MVP) Award.

Over the next decade with the Dodgers, Robinson helped his team win the National League pennant several times. He was a solid hitter, outstanding base stealer, and a great defensive player. In 1955, Robinson and the Dodgers won baseball's top prize, the World Series.

Eventually, Robinson began to speak out about the racist treatment he endured. He protested when he was not allowed to stay in the same hotels or eat in the same restaurants as his teammates. His protests and growing popularity led to policy changes at some hotels and restaurants to allow the integration of blacks and whites.

When Robinson retired in 1957, he had become a hero in baseball. He was voted into the Hall of Fame the first year he was eligible. "Robinson could hit and bunt and steal and run," Roger Kahn wrote in his book *The Boys of Summer*. "He had intimidation skills, and he burned with a dark fire. He wanted passionately to win. He bore the burden of a pioneer and the weight made him stronger. If one can be certain of anything in baseball, it is that we shall not look upon his like again."[32]

Robinson's success in the major leagues opened the door for other black players, including Willie Mays and Hank Aaron. In addition, breaking baseball's color line struck a blow to segregation throughout society. Soon other racial barriers would fall.

Breaking Down the Walls

Following Robinson's historic entry into Major League Baseball, a number of African American athletes broke color barriers in other major sporting leagues. Before 1949, for example, professional basketball teams ignored black athletes. As soon as Robinson made his debut in Major League Baseball, however, professional basketball teams sought black athletes as well.

Several black players recorded basketball firsts in 1950. Chuck Cooper of Duquesne University was the first black player to be drafted. Nat "Sweetwater"

BALL GYMNASTICS

Founded in 1926, the Harlem Globetrotters were one of the first all-black basketball teams. Although known today for their antics and trick shots, the Globetrotters were not always making people laugh on the court. The team barnstormed around the country, playing close to 100 games per year. Their talent led to an impressive record. In 1939, the Globetrotters played in the first national basketball championship, losing to the all-black New York Rens.

Because the Globetrotters could run up a high score on opposing teams, many teams did not want to play them. To encourage their rivals onto the court, the Globetrotters experimented with adding comedy to their games. Trick plays and fancy ball handling helped to slow down the scoring and keep the crowds entertained.

When the National Basketball Association (NBA) began to integrate in the 1950s, opportunities for competitive games for barnstorming teams decreased. In response, the Globetrotters intensified their focus on comedy. Ball gymnastics, rather than strictly competitive play, became their trademark style. Today, the Globetrotters continue to entertain millions of fans all over the world.

Players for the Globetrotters get in some practice on a playground in Chicago in the 1960s.

Clifton signed the first National Basketball Association (NBA) contract with the New York Knickerbockers (Knicks). Earl Lloyd became the first African American to play in an NBA game because his team, the Washington Capitols, played a game before Clifton's debut with the Knicks. Before long, dozens of black athletes filled the rosters of professional basketball teams.

Football was also due for changes. Unlike baseball, football had included a handful of black athletes who played in the first professional football leagues in the 1920s. By 1933, however, white team owners had banded together to ban black players. Unable to play on National Football League (NFL) teams, black football players played on minor league teams or all-black barnstorming teams such as the Harlem Brown Bombers.

However, after the doors opened to African Americans in baseball, football's color line also cracked. In 1946, the NFL's Cleveland Rams moved to Los Angeles. Their stadium contract required that they integrate their team. To comply, the Rams signed two black players, Woody Strode and Kenny Washington. That same year, the Cleveland Browns, a member of the NFL rival All-American Football Conference, signed Marion Motley and Bill Willis.

Although signed in the same year, the four pioneer players had vastly different careers. Injuries ended Washington's career after three seasons, while Strode lasted just one season. In contrast, Willis and Motley enjoyed successful football careers and were inducted into the Pro Football Hall of Fame.

By 1949, three NFL teams had signed black players, and, by 1952, every team except the Washington Redskins had at least one black player. A gradual desegregation of the major sports was underway.

A Higher Standard

Black athletes found themselves in a confusing and ambivalent place during the 1940s and the 1950s. Their skill in sports was admired, and their participation was slowly being accepted. However, when they were not competing, they found themselves less appreciated and more scrutinized. The world watched them carefully and held them to a higher standard than white athletes. Their managers, team owners, and others continually cautioned them to make sure their behavior was spotless.

Black athletes were expected to observe all social norms and to be humble and accommodating, not prideful and outspoken. According to historian John C. Walter, "The well-worn phrase was that these people knew that their behavior on field and off was to be a 'credit to their race.' These men, therefore, had to carry the burden of double circumspection, to play better than white players and also to conduct a life that was far more exemplary than both their white on-the-field counterparts and the ordinary white citizen."[33]

However, as the color lines in professional sports began cracking in the 1950s, raising the positive visibility of African Americans, it gave the black community a platform to become

The world of sports was not the only area experiencing desegregation in the 1950s. Shown here are black students under National Guard protection as they leave their integrated school in Arkansas in 1957.

more vocal for change in other areas. Black papers and communities called for equal voting rights. They wanted access to the same public places, the same schools, and the same job and housing opportunities as whites.

A major step toward civil rights equality occurred with two Supreme Court decisions. In 1953, in *Terry v. Adams*, blacks were given the right to vote in primaries and all elections. The next year, in *Brown v. Board of Education of Topeka*, the Court banned segregation of schools by race. This decision sent shock waves across the country and angered southern whites. Tensions came to a head in Little Rock, Arkansas. When officials tried to integrate a high school there, they met resistance from white mobs and government officials. Images of the violence in Little Rock dominated newspapers and television reports. Eventually, President Dwight D. Eisenhower sent federal troops to Little Rock to take control and regain peace. Although Little Rock had calmed, the civil rights movement was just beginning.

CHAPTER FOUR
WITH RACKETS AND CLUBS

While a number of sports slowly began to integrate following World War II, others were slower to respond. In golf and tennis, for example, administrators and players were much more reluctant to relax their rules and their long history of being white-only sports.

Not Just Caddies

Golf originated in Scotland and came to America with some of the earliest European colonists. In the 1880s, however, golf's popularity soared, and many clubs were established for players. At first, black athletes were allowed to compete, and African American John Shippen Jr. was one of the earliest professional golfers in the United States.

In 1896, 16-year-old Shippen, a former caddie, entered the United States Golf Association's U.S. Open tournament at the new Shinnecock

Hills Golf Club in New York. When white golfers discovered that Shippen was scheduled to play, they threatened to boycott the tournament. However, Theodore Havemeyer, the association's president, supported Shippen's right to play. He announced that the Open would take place even if Shippen and Oscar Bunn, a Native American golfer, were the only two playing.

As a result, Shippen and Bunn became the first American-born golfers to play in the Open. In that event, Shippen tied for fifth place. Over the rest of his career, he golfed in four more U.S. Open tournaments.

However, in 1916, the U.S. Golf Association adopted a new policy stating that blacks could no longer play. Many golf courses would not even allow blacks on the property—unless they were there to work as caddies. Clifford Roberts, one of the founders of the Augusta National Golf Club in Georgia, stated in 1933, "As long as I'm alive, all the golfers will be white and all the caddies will be black."[34] By 1939, with more than 5,000 golf courses in the United States, less than 20 of them allowed blacks to play. Instead, they were relegated to being caddies and assistants.

In 1926, Robert Hawkins formed the United Golf Association (UGA), a professional league for black golfers. Although they were restricted to playing on the few courses that allowed them, the UGA developed a number of male and female golfing stars. One was Althea Gibson, a former tennis star who turned to golf in the 1960s. In 1963, she became the first black woman to be admitted to the Ladies Professional Golf Association (LPGA).

Against the Rules

One of the greatest black golfers of the 1940s was Ted Rhodes, who dominated the UGA tour. He caught the attention of heavyweight boxing champion Joe Louis, who hired Rhodes as his personal golf instructor. Because of Rhodes's graceful golf swing, Louis nicknamed him "Sweet Swinger."

"Teddy was a fantastic golfer," said Lee Elder, who, in 1975, became the first African American to play in the prestigious Masters Golf Tournament. "His game was ... so straight that you could draw an arrow [with it]. His iron game was probably the best that I'll ever see."[35]

At the time, the Professional Golfers' Association (PGA) had rules stating that only whites could be members and play in PGA tournaments. Black golfers like Rhodes knew about the clause. They also knew that some major tournaments had different rules. The Los Angeles Open, the Canadian Open, and the Tam O'Shanter World Championship of Golf in Chicago allowed any qualified player to enter, regardless of race. Rhodes knew he could prove his talent against the world's best golfers in these events.

In 1948, Rhodes entered the Los Angeles Open and finished strong in 20th place. The PGA's tour rules stated that the top 60 golfers would automatically qualify to play in another PGA tournament, the Richmond Open in California. The Richmond Open had traditionally been only accessible to whites. Now, Rhodes and another black golfer, Bill Spiller, who had also qualified, headed to Richmond.

After finishing a practice round at Richmond Country Club, Spiller,

Teddy Rhodes (left) joined fellow golfer Charlie Sifford (center), after Sifford won a Negro golf tournament in 1958. Presenting the trophy is singer and celebrity Nat King Cole.

Rhodes, and Madison Gunter, a local black amateur golfer, learned that they would not be allowed to play in the tournament because they were not members of the PGA—which refused to accept black members.

Changing Policies

Frustrated at not being allowed to play, Spiller and Rhodes filed a $315,000 lawsuit against the Richmond Country Club and the PGA of America. The suit claimed that the two men were being denied their right to earn a living as professional golfers because of their race. It also claimed that the PGA was an establishment that prevented nonunion members from joining, which was illegal under the 1947 Taft-Hartley Act. A hearing was scheduled for September 1948. A few days before the hearing, the PGA offered to allow blacks to play in PGA tournaments if Spiller and Rhodes dropped the lawsuit.

The two golfers agreed to do so—but soon found out that they had been tricked. The PGA changed the tournaments from "opens," in which anyone could play, to "invitationals," accessible only to players who had been specifically invited to compete. Predictably, no black player received an invitation.

When the PGA also banned Joe Louis from the San Diego Open in 1952, the public became more aware of golf's ongoing policies of discrimination. Louis had been invited to be part of the tournament to bring attention to it, and now he was being excluded. Newspapers around the country picked up the story. By the end of the week, the PGA announced that while it would still not allow blacks to become members, it would no longer keep them from playing in events if they were invited and qualified.

Eliminating the Clause

After the 1952 San Diego Open, some tournaments did offer invitations to black golfers. However, the discrimination continued in other ways. When Rhodes and several other black golfers were invited to qualify in the Phoenix Open, they were paired together, since many white players refused to have a black partner. When they teed off on the first hole, they discovered that someone had filled the first hole's cup with human feces. Nonetheless, Rhodes played well, refusing to let the incident upset his game. "Teddy told me that to get angry was the equivalent of losing your game," said Maggie Hathaway, a former golf writer and editor for the black-owned weekly

MOVING THE NEEDLE

In late 2018, the PGA of America, the largest golf organization in the country, issued a statement saying that it wanted to become more diverse. At the time, the group's 29,000 members were 91 percent white and 96 percent male. However, research has shown that a new generation is beginning to change these trends. In 2018, more than 50,000 boys and girls around the country participated in PGA junior leagues. Statistics showed that 15 percent of the players came from diverse ethnic backgrounds, and 25 percent of the players were female.

In 2022, the PGA headquarters will be relocated to the Dallas-Fort Worth section of Texas. Sandy Cross, senior director of diversity and inclusion for the PGA of America, said she thought the move would be helpful in opening up membership. "I think the multicultural population there ... really gives us such an opportunity to further increase the diversity, all dimensions of diversity on our staff."[1] Seth Waugh, chief executive of the PGA of America added, "Dallas is a major city, a diverse, growing, young place, right? So we think it'll naturally ... create more energy and surround the association. Frankly, I would much prefer to have much ... more diversity in our ranks, right? ... Sadly, it takes a lot of time to move the needle."[2]

1. Quoted in Karen Robinson-Jacobs, "With Nearly All-White Membership, PGA of America Looks to Diversify," Dallas News, December 9, 2018. www.dallasnews.com/business/sports-business/2018/12/09/nearly-white-membership-pga-america-looks-diversify.

2. Quoted in Robinson-Jacobs, "With Nearly All-White Membership."

Los Angeles Sentinel. "Getting angry made him so nervous that sometimes he drew his putter back and couldn't bring it forward."[36]

Rhodes played wherever he could for the rest of the 1950s. He eventually made it into 69 PGA events, where he finished in the top 20 a total of 9 times. In 1957, he won the National Negro Open title for the second time. He also became a mentor and coach for future black golfing stars.

When the PGA finally eliminated its whites-only clause in 1961, it was too late for Rhodes. He was in poor health and died in 1969. Forty years later, in 2009, the PGA of America bestowed posthumous membership upon Rhodes, Shippen, and Spiller. "If not for the mere color of their skin, these gentlemen would have most certainly become PGA members in their time," said past PGA president Jim Remy. "While we can never erase the past, we can do everything possible to advance the promise of diversity and hope for all."[37]

A Net Win

Like golf, tennis came into popularity in the United States in the late 19th century, along with the same resistance to integrating black players. While a number of African Americans played the game in its early years, in the early 20th century, the United States Lawn Tennis Association (USLTA) refused to admit African Americans to most of its events. As a result, a group of black tennis enthusiasts formed the American Tennis Association (ATA) in 1916. It became the first black sports organization in the United States.

The ATA developed its own playing circuit and held its first national championships at Baltimore's Druid Hill Park in August 1917. Because blacks were denied lodging at most hotels, the ATA held many of its early events at various black colleges, which provided housing and tennis courts. Soon, the ATA national championship became a highly anticipated social event for the black community. During tournament week, participants and spectators looked forward to dances, fashion shows, and other activities.

The color barrier in tennis began cracking in 1940, when the first interracial match was played. Don Budge, a white player, faced ATA champion Jimmy McDaniel in an exhibition match. Although Budge defeated McDaniel, he complimented the ATA champ. "Jimmy is a very good player, I'd say he'd rank with the first 10 of our white players."[38] Despite the match, tennis would remain mostly segregated until a young woman named Althea Gibson captured the nation's attention in 1950.

"Play, Play, Play"

Born in 1927, Gibson moved with her family from South Carolina to Harlem, New York, as a toddler. As a child she loved to play sports. "I just wanted to play, play, play,"[39] she said. At first, Gibson excelled at paddle tennis, a game that is similar to tennis, but is played with a solid paddle on a smaller court. She developed a reputation for crushing her opponents and soon moved to court tennis, which was better suited to the hard-hitting Gibson. Her intense play earned her

Gibson played at Wimbledon in 1956. The next year, she became the first African American to win the singles title at the prestigious event.

THE WILLIAMS SISTERS

Two of the biggest tennis stars in the world are African American sisters Serena and Venus Williams. The girls began their training while still in elementary school, and their hours of hard work paid off. By early 2019, the two of them had won 30 Grand Slam singles titles and more than $120 million in prize money. Only a year apart in age, they often find themselves competing against each other.

Despite the fact that they are competing decades after people like Althea Gibson, the sisters still face racial insults and discrimination. Katrina Adams, the African American president and CEO of the U.S. Tennis Association, recently stated, "Every time we step on the court, we are carrying the weight of an entire society of people and trying to accomplish things. Talking about breaking the glass ceilings, any time that we are trying to accomplish or achieve anything, we have to work twice as hard."[1]

Sarah Jackson, a Northeastern University professor, added, "When a black player like Althea Gibson or Arthur Ashe or Serena Williams becomes dominant, that in and of itself is political. They might not themselves be intentionally making a political statement. But there's no way to avoid the fact that what they're doing balks the norms of race and racism of the sport and of the society."[2]

1. Quoted in Alex Schroeder, "Serena Williams and the Inherent Politics of Tennis," WBUR, August 29, 2018. www.wbur.org/onpoint/2018/08/29/serena-williams-tennis-racism-sexism-politics.

2. Quoted in Schroeder, "Serena Williams."

a spot at the Cosmopolitan Tennis Club in Harlem. The club was home to elite black tennis players. Amazed by Gibson's power and skill, club members sponsored her junior club membership. Within a year, Gibson's training paid off and she won the ATA's junior championship.

In 1946, Gibson's play attracted the attention of two southern doctors, Hubert Eaton and Robert Johnson, who were active in the black tennis community. They recognized Gibson's talent but knew that she needed additional training. The doctors became her patrons, and, after getting her parents' permission, she spent the school year with the Eatons and the

Sisters Serena (left) and Venus (right) Williams often find themselves on the tennis court together—sometimes as partners and sometimes as opponents.

summer with the Johnsons. With the doctors' mentoring and connections, Gibson had access to top-notch instruction and competitions. She graduated from high school and attended college at Florida A&M on a tennis and basketball scholarship.

By age 20, Gibson had won 10 consecutive ATA national championships. Despite her talent, the USLTA at first refused to let her compete with white players in the 1950 U.S. Nationals. Then, Alice Marble, a four-time winner of the event, wrote a scathing commentary in the July 1950 issue of *American Lawn Tennis* magazine. "If Althea Gibson represents a challenge to the present crop of players, then it's only fair that they meet this challenge on the courts,"[40] she wrote. The USLTA relented and allowed the Orange Lawn Tennis Club in New Jersey to invite Gibson to the 1950 Eastern Grass Court championships. Gibson did not win, but she earned a bid to the U.S. Nationals at Forest Hills in Queens, New York. At her debut there, Gibson advanced to a historic match against the Wimbledon singles champion, Louise Brough. Although Gibson lost, she proved that she could play with the best. The next year, the USLTA invited her to play at Wimbledon, which is one of the most famous tournaments in tennis.

Gibson went on to win her first major tennis tournament at the 1956 French Open. In 1957, she won her first Wimbledon singles title. Recalling her preparation for the tournament, Gibson said, "I was ruthless on the tennis court. Win at any cost, I became an attacker. If your first serve ain't good, I'll knock it down your throat."[41] She also won the U.S. Nationals in the same year. During her career, Gibson won five Grand Slam singles titles and six doubles titles.

Even though Gibson had broken into formerly whites-only tennis tournaments, she still experienced difficulties because of her skin color.

Sometimes hotels denied her a room. One time, a hotel refused to book her a reservation for a luncheon that was being held in her honor.

On the larger stage, however, many chose to celebrate her accomplishments. In 1957 and 1958, the Associated Press voted Gibson the Female Athlete of the Year. She was the first black woman to receive the honor. Gibson retired from tennis in 1958, going on to try her hand at singing, acting, and golf, where she became the first black player on the LPGA tour.

Gibson will always be remembered as the tennis pioneer who paved the way for future African American tennis greats. Tennis star Billie Jean King, winner of 12 Grand Slam singles titles, said, "If it hadn't been for her, it wouldn't have been so easy for Arthur (Ashe) or the ones who followed."[42]

From Bookworm to Champion

Despite Gibson's accomplishments, it was almost a decade before another African American tennis player rose to the top. A player named Arthur Ashe changed the history of tennis with his skill and determination. Born in 1943, Ashe was an unlikely athletic star. As a child, he was a shy, uncoordinated bookworm. "I was too

*Arthur Ashe was a dominant tennis player for years,
often making last-minute backhand returns such as this one.*

small for any sport but tennis," he said. "I learned to swim when I was very young, but I was always a bit afraid of water. My father wouldn't let me play football because of my size."[43]

Ashe learned to play tennis in Richmond, Virginia's Brookfield Park. There, he attracted the attention of Ronald Charity, a tennis player and coach. Charity was impressed with the young man and arranged for him to meet with Robert Johnson, who years earlier had coached and mentored Althea Gibson. In 1953,

Johnson took Ashe to his home for the summer. He tutored young black men and women, including Ashe, and helped them earn tennis college scholarships. With Johnson's coaching, Ashe's game grew stronger.

In 1955, Ashe won his first tournament, a singles event for boys 12 and under. Three years later, he was the first African American to play in the Maryland boys' championship. As Ashe continued racking up ATA titles in the late 1950s and early 1960s, people began to notice him. In 1965, he leaped onto the national stage

TWO TENNIS GREATS

In 2019, a documentary called *Althea & Arthur* was released on the CBS Sports Network during Black History Month. Narrated by actress Phylicia Rashad, it explored the impact both athletes had on tennis and on the advancement of civil rights in America. The tennis stars and their family members are featured in the film, along with a group of girls from a tennis group in North Carolina. These girls campaigned to get a statue of Gibson installed at the Billie Jean King Tennis Center in New York. After studying the revolutionary tennis player, the 6th and 7th grade girls were shocked to find out there was no permanent memorial of her, explained Lenny Simpson, a tennis pro who organized the non-profit group in order to help disadvantaged kids through tennis. "I thought it was disrespectful there wasn't a monument," said student Destiny Gieschen. "She did so much for African-Americans and women."[1]

1. Quoted in Ben Steelman, "Wilmington Youths Help Gain Statue for Althea Gibson," Star News Online, March 23, 2018. www.starnewsonline.com/news/20180323/wilmington-youths-help-gain-statue-for-althea-gibson.

when he won the National Collegiate Athletic Association (NCAA) title while a student at UCLA. While winning on the court, Ashe still experienced the sting of discrimination. In college, he was once asked to sit out of a tournament because black players were not allowed to enter.

In 1968, Ashe won the U.S. Open. Later that year, he was the first African American to be invited to play on the U.S. Davis Cup team. Ashe won 35 amateur singles titles before he went pro and then triumphed with an additional 33 singles titles, including the 1970 Australian Open and Wimbledon in 1975.

In a game dominated by white players, Ashe used his status as a black star to speak out about causes he supported. He pushed to create inner-city tennis programs for underprivileged kids and helped found the Association of Tennis Professionals.

In addition, he frequently protested South Africa's system of apartheid, which privileged whites and denied rights to blacks. Although Ashe had become a world-renowned tennis star, the South African government

Former New York City mayor David Dinkins displays an award dedicated to Althea Gibson at the 2004 U.S. Open Tennis Tournament.

denied him a visa to play in the 1969 South African Open. Ashe protested, and in 1973, he finally received a visa to play in South Africa. He became the first black player to win a title in the country. "You have shown our black youth that they can compete with whites and win,"[44] said African poet Don Mattera.

Ashe's tennis career ended prematurely when he suffered a heart attack in 1979. He retired in 1980, and 12 years later, he announced that he had contracted a deadly disease known as acquired immunodeficiency syndrome (AIDS) from a blood transfusion. He died in 1993.

Ashe was one of the most notable tennis players of his time, but he is also remembered for the causes he championed both on and off the tennis court. In fact, he was one of many black athletes who chose to use their fame, reputation, and influence to promote equality for the African American community.

CHAPTER FIVE
USING THEIR VOICES

In the 1960s, the United States was immersed in the growing battle for civil rights. Despite new laws and court rulings, in practice, equal rights for blacks were still out of reach. The African American community challenged this ongoing racial injustice with intensity and determination. In the past, black athletes had been cautioned—even required—not to talk about sensitive racial issues. Some, like Arthur Ashe, pushed back and used their status to speak out against the intolerance and prejudice that they and so many others faced on a daily basis. Their brave actions and heartfelt words inspired other athletes, as well as ordinary citizens, to focus and unite as they fought for the rights every person deserved.

A Team Player

In the late 1950s and 1960s, one of the greatest basketball defenders was Boston Celtics center Bill Russell. He led his team to an amazing 11 titles in 13 seasons. Russell's aggressive defensive style revolutionized how basketball was played. He swooped across the court, blocked shots, and rebounded balls. His career average of 22.5 rebounds per game stands as the second highest of all time. "I was an innovator," Russell said. "I started blocking shots although I had never seen a shot blocked before that."[45]

Born in 1934 in Louisiana, Russell moved with his family to California as a child. As a teen, he stood more than six feet tall, but he showed little athletic skill on the basketball court. He was cut from his junior high basketball team, but a high school coach decided to take a chance on him. "I believe that man saved me from becoming a juvenile delinquent," wrote Russell in his first autobiography, *Go Up for Glory*.

Bill Russell (center) was known for speaking about issues of discrimination. In July 1964, he spoke during a press conference for the National Association for the Advancement of Colored People (NAACP), an organization formed in 1909 to promote civil rights for blacks.

Frustrated and angered by seeing his parents face daily discrimination, he wrote, "If I hadn't had basketball, all my energies and frustrations would surely have been carried in some other direction."[46] Russell did not start on his high school team until his senior year. He then displayed his unique style of jumping to block shots, something that had never been seen before.

Only one college offered Russell a basketball scholarship—the University of San Francisco (USF). African American players were still rare in college basketball, and Russell's USF team became the first to have three black players as starters. In college, Russell exploded on the court and became a dominating center. During his time at USF, the team won two consecutive NCAA championships and had a string of 60 consecutive wins.

Such accomplishments did not make him immune to the discrimination still used against black players. Crowds yelled insults at him and his black teammates. During the 1955 All-College tournament in Oklahoma City, one hotel refused to allow Russell and his black teammates to book a room. In protest, the entire USF team chose to stay in an empty college dormitory instead.

Red Auerbach, the coach of the Boston Celtics, noticed Russell and thought his defensive skills were just what the Celtics needed to win a championship. He selected Russell in the 1956 NBA draft. Russell did not join the Celtics until the middle of the 1956–1957 season, however—first he went to the 1956 Olympics in Melbourne, Australia, where he helped the U.S. basketball team take home a gold medal.

Russell dominated on the court, and, with his presence, the Celtics began to win. They won their first NBA championship in 1957. Over the next 13 years, they won 11 titles, including an unmatched streak of 8 consecutive championships. During that time, Russell was named the NBA's MVP five times.

Leading off the Court

Even when the Celtics were at their peak, Russell struggled against discrimination. There were many empty seats in the Boston Garden where the Celtics played, while less successful teams sold out their arenas. Some white Boston sportswriters refused to vote for him as the most valuable player because he was black. When Russell bought a house in a white Boston suburb, neighbors harassed and threatened him, and one time, vandals broke into his home and marked the walls with graffiti.

In spite of the threats, Russell was determined to use his public spotlight to support the civil rights movement. Even though he knew it would damage his popularity with white fans, he joined civil rights activist and minister Martin Luther King Jr. in the 1963 March on Washington for Jobs and Freedom, and he spoke out against the Vietnam War.

When Celtics coach Auerbach moved to the team's front office in 1966, the team named Russell—who was still playing—as his replacement. Russell became the first black coach for a major professional sports team in the United States. At a press conference announcing the move, a reporter asked Russell if he could coach the white players without being prejudiced. "Now, I didn't recall anybody asking a white coach if he could coach the black guys without being prejudiced. All I said was, 'Yeah,'"[47] Russell later remembered.

In the spring of 1968, King was assassinated. Many, especially in the African American community, were

OUTLAWING DISCRIMINATION

Enacted on July 2, 1964, the Civil Rights Act of 1964 outlawed major forms of discrimination against blacks and women in the United States. The act outlawed racial segregation in schools, at workplaces, and in public facilities. It also ended unequal application of voter registration requirements.

President Lyndon B. Johnson signed the bill in a nationwide television broadcast. Before signing, he said,

We believe that all men are created equal. Yet many are denied equal treatment.

We believe that all men have certain inalienable rights. We believe that all men are entitled to the blessings of liberty. Yet millions are being deprived of those blessings. Not because of their own failures, but because of the color of their skin. The reasons are deeply embedded in history and tradition and the nature of man. We can understand without rancor or hatred how all this happens. But it cannot continue. Our Constitution, the foundation of our Republic, forbids it. The principles of our freedom forbid it. Morality forbids it. And the law I sign tonight forbids it.[1]

1. Quoted in "Radio Coverage of President's Johnson's Remarks upon Signing the Civil Rights Act of 1964: The Complete Speech," Library of Congress, accessed on April 30, 2019. www.loc.gov/exhibits/civil-rights-act/multimedia/johnson-signing-remarks.html.

distraught and angry over King's violent death. Russell vocally supported the rights of African Americans to defend themselves against racial violence, not caring how his opinions might affect his public image.

After winning his 11th championship in the 1969 finals, Russell retired from the Celtics. In 1972, the Celtics retired Russell's jersey, and three years later, he was inducted into the Basketball Hall of Fame. However, he did not attend the ceremonies for either event, instead issuing a statement that he did not want to be inducted. Years later, Russell explained that he did not want to be connected with certain members of the Hall of Fame, particularly

Adolph Rupp, who had been a long-time coach at the University of Kentucky. Russell felt Rupp was a racist who supported segregated sports. "I did not want to be associated with him or anyone else of his racial views. I saw that as my free choice to make,"[48] Russell wrote. Shunning his own induction brought harsh criticism from many people, yet Russell demonstrated once again his willingness to stand up for his beliefs no matter what others said. "Bill Russell got tagged with being antiwhite and rude and everything else," said former teammate Tommy Heinsohn. "But all he really wanted to do was be recognized as an individual. He had been slighted several times, and he was smart enough to recognize it."[49]

Since his retirement, Russell has continued to be an active voice for civil rights. He has partnered with the NBA and the U.S. government to hold basketball clinics in more than 50 countries on 6 continents. He also was the first winner of the NBA's Civil Rights Award. In 2011, President Barack Obama praised Russell's efforts and awarded him the Presidential Medal of Freedom, the nation's highest civilian honor.

Gridiron Star

Many football fans agree that Jim Brown was one of the greatest running backs of all time. During his nine-year career with the Cleveland Browns in the 1950s and 1960s, he did more than run; he caught passes, returned kickoffs, and even threw touchdown passes. Over his career, Brown accumulated 12,312 rushing yards and 15,459 combined net yards. He played in nine Pro Bowls, one in each year of his career. He also earned the NFL's MVP award four times.

As a teenager, Brown attended Manhasset High School in New York, where he became an athletic standout. During his high school years, a group of white professional men mentored him and encouraged him to study and run for student government.

When Brown began playing football at Syracuse University in New York in 1954, it was an eye-opening experience for him. He was the only African American player on the team, and he encountered more problems with discrimination than he had in high school. "I met all those loving white people at Manhasset. Then I went to Syracuse, ran chin first into overt racism. Someone had changed

Jim Brown wore number 32 during his time in Cleveland.

all the rules, and forgotten to tell me,"[50] he said.

Troubled, Brown said he realized that he was not being judged as an individual but defined by his race. He recalled,

I came up at the crossroads of segregation. There were still colleges where black players couldn't play. There were teams that would go south, and black players had to stay in private homes. It was a blessing [as a black man to be able to play college football] because there were opportunities, but it was demeaning because you were looked on as inferior. It was almost as if you'd been given a favor. And you always felt you had to perform much, much better.[51]

At Syracuse, Brown quickly became a star in four sports and earned All-American honors. In 1957, the NFL's Cleveland Browns selected Brown as their number one draft pick. With his strength, speed, and agility, he quickly became the premier running back in the league. Brown said,

But you could never just play and not be cognizant of the social situation in the country. Every day of

your life, that was in your mind. You had to question why they only put black players at certain positions, why there were positions that blacks weren't smart enough to play ... So I was very conscious of the civil-rights movement and very active in what I call the movement for dignity, equality and justice. In fact, it superseded my interest in sports. Sports gave me an opportunity to help the cause.[52]

Brown used his status as a football star to speak out about racism in sports and society. Although he made many people uncomfortable, others respected his honesty. "Please keep talking," wrote one St. Louis man. "Even though your words hurt, they may open some eyes and change some actions while there's time."[53]

Brown shocked football fans when he retired in 1966 at the peak of his career, leaving the sport as the NFL's all-time leading rusher. After his retirement, Brown pursued a career in acting, as well as mentoring athletes. He also worked in the community to help rehabilitate gang members and prisoners, and he went on to be a special advisor for the Cleveland Browns.

From Clay to Ali

Born in 1942 in Kentucky, Cassius Clay Jr. started boxing around the age of 12, and at 16 won the Louisville Golden Gloves light heavyweight title. After high school, Clay won his second National Amateur Athletic Union title and traveled to Rome, Italy, to represent the United States in the 1960 Olympic Games, where he won the gold medal.

After he returned home, Clay hired a trainer and began fighting professionally. With a flair for showmanship, Clay announced before each fight in which round he would win. Amazingly, his predictions often came true. His entertaining style attracted growing audiences. He was undefeated after 19 professional fights, winning 15 of them by knockout. Finally, on February 25, 1964, he got his chance at the heavyweight title with a match against reigning champ Sonny Liston.

Before the fight, most boxing experts did not give the 22-year-old Clay a chance against the more experienced Liston. One of Clay's advisors told him to "float like a butterfly, sting like a bee," a phrase that will always be associated with Clay. Clay's quick feet and stinging fists proved to be too much for the slower Liston. Clay won in six rounds.

"I am the greatest,"[54] Clay shouted after the win, becoming the youngest heavyweight champion in history. Shortly after winning, Clay stunned the world when he announced that he was a member of the Nation of Islam, an African American militant religious group that supported violent civil rights protests but also believed in separation of the races. He also took a new name to reflect his new religion: Now, he would be known as Muhammad Ali.

By announcing his allegiance to the group, the popular boxer immediately became one of the country's most controversial figures. Many people were confused and angry that their sports hero was now supporting a group that shunned Christianity and openly criticized whites.

Even black Americans were disturbed by Ali's announcement. Christianity had been a strong pillar of faith in the black community for decades. Many did not support Ali's decision; however, they respected him for standing up for his beliefs.

A Controversial Stand

In 1966, the U.S. military drafted Ali during the Vietnam War. Ali, along with other members of the Nation of Islam, did not support the war. He requested to be excused from military duty because of his religious beliefs. The U.S. government denied the request and ordered him to report for service. Ali refused and issued a statement saying, "I have searched my conscience and I find I cannot be true to my belief in my religion by accepting such a call."[55]

His decision had far-reaching consequences. Immediately, boxing organizations stripped the champ of his heavyweight crown and revoked his boxing license. The U.S. government indicted him and found him guilty of draft evasion in 1967. He was fined $10,000 and sentenced to five years in prison. Ali appealed the ruling. In 1971, the U.S. Supreme Court overturned the conviction. It ruled that Ali's objection to the war was based on legitimate religious beliefs. Four years after being banned from boxing, Ali was free to resume his career.

Returning to the boxing ring, Ali challenged undefeated Joe Frazier in the "Fight of the Century" in 1971. The match lasted 15 rounds before Frazier knocked out Ali. It was Ali's first professional loss. Three years later, in 1974, Ali won in a rematch against Frazier. Also in 1974, Ali regained his heavyweight crown by beating reigning champ George Foreman in the "Rumble in

Sonny Liston stayed down for the count after Ali knocked him out in a fight in 1965.

President George W. Bush presented Muhammad Ali with the Presidential Medal of Freedom at the White House in 2005.

the Jungle," a match staged in Zaire (today's Democratic Republic of the Congo). In 1975, Ali battled Frazier for a third time, this time in a match-up dubbed the "Thrilla in Manila." Held in the Philippines, many consider it to be the greatest boxing match of all time. Ali won again. By the late 1970s, Ali's career began to decline, and he lost several bouts. He retired in 1981.

In 1984, Ali announced that he had Parkinson's disease, a degenerative neurological disorder. Over the years, the disease robbed him of the graceful movements he had shown in the boxing ring. Despite his health challenges, Ali spent much of his time supporting charitable causes, traveling all over the world to help those less fortunate. In 1998, he was chosen to be a United Nations Messenger of Peace because of his work. In addition, in 2005, Ali received the Presidential Medal of Freedom from President George W. Bush.

Ali died in 2016 at the age of 74. Reverend Kevin Cosby, a friend of the fighter who spoke at Ali's funeral, stated, "Everything in American history was designed to infuse in black people that we were nobody. But then, here comes Ali. And during a time when black people had been taught that they were nobody, here is a man who taught black people that they were somebody."[56]

Boycotts and Protests

As sports stars like Russell, Brown, and Ali made headlines, the civil rights movement continued to grow throughout the United States. African Americans were growing increasingly impatient, tired of waiting for the government to take action on essential civil rights issues. At last, they decided to take matters into their own hands. They organized sit-ins and protests to push for integration of public places like lunch counters, beaches, and libraries. In the beginning, these demonstrations were peaceful, but that changed as the protests spread into the South, where protesters often faced angry insults, bomb threats, and physical violence.

During these volatile times, black athletes found themselves more empowered than ever to use their status to call attention to civil rights causes. In 1968, the Olympic Games were scheduled to be held in Mexico. The International Olympic Committee (IOC) planned to allow South African athletes to participate in the Games, a decision that outraged many because of the country's system of apartheid.

In protest, Harry Edwards, a sociology professor at San Diego State University, called for African American athletes to boycott the Games. Star athletes Russell, Brown, and Ali publicly supported the plan. Their star power brought more attention to the proposed boycott. Eventually, more than 30 countries joined the call for a boycott. This got the IOC's attention, and it banned South Africa. After this move, U.S. black athletes decided to compete.

In addition to competing, some African American athletes used the international stage for individual protests. In the 200-meter race, sprinters Tommie Smith and John Carlos won the gold and bronze medals, respectively. When they arrived at the medal ceremony, the two men wore black socks and no shoes to symbolize African American poverty, as well as a black glove to represent the community's strength and unity. Smith wore a scarf and Carlos wore beads, in remembrance of lynching victims. As they stood on the medal podium during the playing of the U.S. national anthem, the two men bowed their heads and raised a clenched fist. This image was broadcast to an international television audience. "It was a polarizing moment because it was seen as an example of black power

radicalism," said Doug Hartmann, a University of Minnesota sociologist. "Mainstream America hated what they did."[57]

Olympic officials swiftly reacted to the athletes' protest. They banned Smith and Carlos from the remainder of the Games. The men returned to the United States where reaction to their protest was mixed. Democratic vice presidential nominee Edmund Muskie told the press that the men probably should not have made the black power statement at the Olympics. On the other hand, baseball great Jackie Robinson criticized the U.S. Olympic Committee for banning Smith and Carlos. "The Olympic Committee made a grave mistake in suspending them. I take pride in their proudness in being black. What they did had nothing to do with shaming this country,"[58] he said. Regardless of public opinion, the moment became one of the most enduring symbols of how athletes had tied themselves to the civil rights movement.

In 2019, Carlos reflected on the decision he and Smith had made decades earlier and encouraged people to continue to protest against injustice and to influence change. "I would tell them, get in touch with the man in the mirror, the woman in the mirror," he advised. "We have to come together

Smith and Carlos, their fists raised in what was thought of as the black power salute, are shown here.

POWERFUL WORDS

During the 2016 ESPY Awards, given for excellence in sports performance, African American NBA stars LeBron James, Carmelo Anthony, Chris Paul, and Dwyane Wade took their moment in the spotlight to make a statement about racism and ask for change. They were there, as Anthony said, "because we cannot ignore the realities of the current state of America ... The system is broken." He continued, "The problems are not new. The violence is not new. And the racial divide definitely is not new. But the urgency to create change is at an all-time high."[1]

Paul focused on the importance of continuing the legacy of those who had come before: "Generations ago, legends like Jesse Owens, Jackie Robinson, Muhammad Ali, John Carlos, and Tommie Smith, Kareem Abdul-Jabbar, Jim Brown, Billie Jean King, Arthur Ashe, and countless others, they set a model for what athletes should stand for. So we choose to follow in their footsteps."[2]

James encouraged his sports colleagues to use the moment as a "call to action for all professional athletes to educate [themselves.]" He said, "Speak up. Use our influence. And renounce all violence."[3]

1. Quoted in Melissa Chan, "Read LeBron James and Carmelo Anthony's Powerful Speech on Race at the ESPY Awards," *TIME*, July 14, 2016. time.com/4406289/lebron-james-carmelo-anthony-espy-awards-transcript/.

2. Quoted in Chan, "Read LeBron James."

3. Quoted in Chan, "Read LeBron James."

and realize we are all a significant part of this puzzle and everybody is supposed to do their part."[59]

Taking a Knee

Despite some gains, fair and equal treatment of African Americans is still a problem, and the era of protests has not ended. In some ways, these protests have become even more conspicuous and more widespread. Some sports champions are refusing to accept congratulatory invitations to the White House in order to show their dislike of government officials or policies. Other black athletes are using their moments on stage to speak about their personal beliefs and encourage action.

During the 2016 ESPY Awards, NBA stars spoke out for change.

In 2016, San Francisco 49ers quarterback Colin Kaepernick did something that tore through social media like wildfire. Before a game on September 1, as the national anthem began to play, the football player went down on one knee and stayed there throughout the song. When asked why he did it, he replied, "I am not going to stand up to show pride in a flag for a country that oppresses black people and people of color. To me," he continued, "this is bigger than football and it would be selfish on my part to look the other way."[60]

It did not take long for other players—on other NFL teams

Colin Kaepernick inspired many people, such as those shown here, with his decision to kneel to protest racial injustice. However, he also outraged others.

and in other sports—to follow Kaepernick's lead and start taking a knee. It was their way to make nonviolent statements about continuing instances of racial injustice, especially involving police brutality against African Americans. Some people were incensed, calling for any player who kneeled to be suspended, while others thought it was an excellent way to protest nonviolently. President Obama supported the players' rights to protest, while his successor, Donald Trump, spoke out against the practice and demanded for it to end.

CHAPTER SIX
MAKING HISTORY, CHANGING MINDS

When Tony Dungy and Lovie Smith stepped onto the field for Super Bowl XLI in February 2007, they made history even before the first play. Dungy, the head coach of the Indianapolis Colts, and Smith, head coach of the Chicago Bears, together became the first African American head coaches in the NFL's biggest game. A few hours later, Dungy made history again when the Colts defeated the Bears. When the first Super Bowl was played in 1967, many would have thought it impossible for a black man to lead a Super Bowl championship team. Yet, on one of the biggest stages in sports, Dungy and Smith proved that excellence comes in many colors.

In the years since the height of the civil rights era, African American athletes have continued to excel in both professional and college sports. The numbers of black athletes in professional leagues has increased significantly, as have incomes, with African American athletes earning as much as or more than their white teammates. In addition, a significant number of African American athletes have received lucrative endorsement contracts for products ranging from breakfast cereals to automobiles. Only 50 years earlier, the idea of an African American athlete on the cover of a cereal box would have been unthinkable.

In the past few decades, sports have become increasingly integrated. According to a 2018 report by the Institute for Diversity and Ethics in Sport at the University of Central Florida, African American men represent 44.8 percent of football players and 53.6 percent of basketball players in Division I, the highest level in college sports. In addition, college football's most coveted individual honor, the Heisman Trophy, has been awarded to six African American players in the last decade.

The trend has carried into the major professional leagues, where more African American athletes are getting roster slots. In the NBA, approximately 75 percent of the league's players are African American—more than in any other professional league. In addition, because many NBA coaches tend to be former players, African Americans are also getting opportunities to continue in sports jobs even when they are no longer playing.

A New Standard

With more opportunities to play, several African American athletes have become superstars in their chosen sports. In 2010, golfer Tiger Woods topped *Sports Illustrated*'s list of top-earning athletes, bringing in $90.5 million from endorsements, salary, and winnings. His image took a hit the previous year for a scandal in his personal life, and he then suffered several injuries that set back his career. However, he rebounded, and he won the 2019 Masters in Augusta, Georgia, his first major win in more than a decade.

Born Eldrick Tont Woods in 1975 to an African American father and Thai mother, Woods began playing golf as a child. By age eight, he was showing off his skills on morning television shows. Woods won a number of U.S. amateur golf titles before turning professional in 1996. At the age of 21, Woods won one of golf's most legendary tournaments, the Masters, the youngest golfer and first African American to do so.

During his time on the course, Woods has won dozens of tournaments. In 2018, he won the Tour Championship on the PGA Tour—his 80th victory! As of 2019, he also held or shared the record for low score in three of golf's four major championships. (In golf, the lower the score, the better.) In 2018, Woods placed in the top 50 players of all time in the Official World Golf Ranking, and in 2019, he was chosen as captain's pick for the U.S. Ryder Cup Team. "He has influenced so many people to pick up the game of golf like no other golfer could and that is just a testament to how good of an ambassador he is for the sport," wrote journalist Jacob Poore. "He may be the greatest golfer of all time, but I believe because of his overall impact on golf and how dominant he was, he is one of the best athletes of all time."[61]

Through a long career of ups and downs, Tiger Woods has proven himself as one of the most talented golfers in the world.

Hoop Success Stories

Some of the most successful African American athletes have made their marks on the basketball court. Two decades after Bill Russell came Michael Jordan, who dominated the NBA from the mid-1980s through the late 1990s. With his gravity-defying slam dunks and acrobatic moves, Jordan led the Chicago Bulls to six national championships. He also accumulated 10 scoring titles, 14 All-Star Game appearances, and 5 NBA Most Valuable Player awards.

Jordan's spectacular play revived waning interest in the NBA. His good looks, charming smile, and hardworking attitude made him likable.

It also helped him become one of the greatest sports marketing success stories in history. When Jordan came to prominence, the powerhouse Nike brand was still a struggling athletic shoe company. Looking for a way to raise its profile, the company paid Jordan to put his name and image on a new brand of shoes, Air Jordans. Propelled by Jordan's rising star status, Air Jordans were a huge success and proved that black athletes could sell products.

Earvin "Magic" Johnson is another of basketball's top 50 players of all time. He played for the Los Angeles Lakers for 12 years and helped them win 5 NBA championships. He was the NBA's MVP three times before retiring in 1991. That year, Johnson was diagnosed with HIV, and he has since dedicated his life to raising awareness of the condition. Along with his radio stations, movie theaters, real estate, and other investments, he is also CEO of the Magic Johnson Foundation, an organization supporting education and prevention of HIV/AIDS.

Other basketball stars that have become familiar faces include retired players Shaquille O'Neal and Charles Barkley, who are frequent analysts on the television show *Inside the NBA*; Stephen Curry, who is a superstar for the Golden State Warriors; and LeBron James, who is sometimes called basketball's best player ever.

Moving Up the Ladder

While African Americans are now accepted in playing positions, their path to coaching, management, and ownership positions in sports has been slower. When Bill Russell was named player-coach of the NBA's Boston Celtics in 1966, it was the first time an African American was considered a legitimate candidate for a coaching or executive position for a major sports team. Other pioneers followed. In 1975, the Cleveland Indians hired Frank Robinson, who became the first black manager in Major League Baseball history. In 1989, Art Shell became the NFL's first African American head coach. Despite these firsts, the coaching ranks of college and professional sports have been slow to integrate African American coaches.

In 2003, the NFL instituted a requirement that teams must interview at least one minority candidate before hiring a head coach. In 2009, the rule was expanded to include the same requirements for hiring team general managers. By 2018, there were eight African American coaches in the NFL—but then six were fired

PAYING IT FORWARD

Named by *Sports Illustrated* as the "Greatest Female Athlete of the 20th Century," Jackie Joyner-Kersee dominated the heptathlon, a seven-event competition consisting of the 100-meter hurdles, high jump, shot put, 200-meter run, 800-meter run, long jump, and javelin. She was the first to score 7,000 in the event, and in 1988, she set the current world record of 7,291 points.

With her strength, speed, and stamina, Joyner-Kersee won the silver medal in the event at the 1984 Olympic Games, losing the gold by less than a second. In the 1988 and 1992 Games, she captured the gold. She also won a gold medal in 1988 and two bronzes in 1992 and 1996 for the long jump. Following her years in track and field, Joyner-Kersee played professional basketball for the Richmond Rage. In 2000, she opened the Jackie Joyner-Kersee Foundation in East St. Louis, Illinois. The after-school center was an area for students to play sports and do homework. As the former runner said, "I think athletes should give back to the community. Some have the idea that no one did anything for them, but if they give back, it helps the next person."[1]

In an interview with *Forbes* magazine, Joyner-Kersee had important advice to give to young people who might be struggling. "Don't let anyone tell you that you can't do something," she said. "You can turn a doubter into a believer as long as *you* believe. It doesn't matter what the people around you are saying, as long as you believe, you will convince people within your circle to also believe." She also said to never give up on yourself. "Be true to who you are,"[2] she stated.

1. Quoted in Tony Paige, "Jackie Joyner-Kersee has Found her Life's Calling Running Foundation for Kinds in her Hometown," *New York Daily News*, February 16, 2019. www.nydailynews.com/sports/more-sports/ny-sports-end-zone-jackie-joyner-kersee-20190215-story.html.

2. Quoted in Jeryl Brunner, "Legendary Track and Field Olympian Jackie Joyner-Kersee Shares the Best Advice She's Ever Gotten," *Forbes*, October 6, 2017. www.forbes.com/sites/jerylbrunner/2017/10/06/legendary-track-and-field-olympian-jackie-joyner-kersee-shares-the-best-advice-shes-ever-gotten/#1f7e12f13c3a.

after turning in poor records. In 2018, roughly a quarter of the NBA's 30 teams had African American coaches, while Major League Baseball had one black manager, Dave Roberts of the Los Angeles Dodgers.

A conference examining the lack of black coaches in the NFL was held

Joyner-Kersee clears a hurdle during an event at the 1988 Olympic Summer Games in Seoul, South Korea.

in the summer of 2019. It brought together young minority coaches with established head coaches to discuss the issue. Troy Vincent, the NFL's vice president of football operations stated, "Coaches tend to hire who they know and who they trust ... That is one of the objectives of the

Michael Jordan's ability to jump high, along with his long reach, made him the most formidable player on the Chicago Bulls—and in the entire NBA.

SELLING IT

Before Michael Jordan signed a Nike deal in 1984, African American athletes had a limited presence in advertising. They appeared in some ads, but they were usually restricted to those targeting the black community. Jordan's commercial success proved that African American athletes could be effective, valuable marketers to people of all races. He paved the way for other African American athletes to sign multi-million-dollar endorsement deals with major companies. "When a corporation sees Michael Jordan, they don't see race. They see him adding $200 million to sales. The color they see is green,"[1] said Brian Murphy, editor and publisher of the Sports Marketing Letter.

Today, talent and achievement are the standards for choosing an endorser, and African American athletes are some of the highest paid out there. They often make more money from their product endorsements than they do playing sports.

1. Quoted in Jon Morgan, "Black Sports Stars Dominate Ads Endorsements," *Baltimore Sun*, February 27, 1998. www.baltimoresun.com/news/bs-xpm-1998-02-27-1998058039-story.html.

---

summit, to expand those horizons and get coaches together with some assistants they do not already know."[62] James Harris, a former quarterback, added, "The hope is that the people there feel a connection with these coaches and feel good about their ability, and go on to endorse them or hire them."[63]

If there is a lack of black coaches, there are even fewer black team owners. As of summer 2019, there are 92 total teams in the NFL, NBA, and MLB. Only one of these teams is owned by an African American— Michael Jordan owns the NBA's Charlotte Hornets—and a handful of other teams are owned by people of other minority groups. No African Americans are majority owners in Major League Baseball, and no African American has ever held a majority ownership interest in an NFL team.

Clearly, there are still higher levels for African Americans to aspire to in sports, but the achievements over the last 150 years have been remarkable. From jockey Isaac Murphy's speed around the racetrack to gymnast Simone Biles's powerful leaps and twists, African American athletes have been amazing people for generations.

Such accomplishments are made

even more impressive when considering how these athletes had to battle for the same basic rights that their white teammates and fans enjoyed, including the opportunity to eat, sleep, live, and work where they chose. Their determination and dedication helped to lay the foundation for those who followed. If not for Althea Gibson, there might not have been the Williams sisters. If not for John Shippen, there might not have been Tiger Woods. Without Jack Johnson, Muhammad Ali might never have been a household name. With each point scored, with each game won, and with each stand taken, these men and women served as symbols of hope, pride, and unity for the entire African American community.

NOTES

Introduction: African American Champions

1. Quoted in Bryan Armen Graham, "Simone Biles: 'Some Days I'm Like, Why Am I Here? But in the End It's All Worth It,'" *Guardian*, August 17, 2018. www.theguardian.com/sport/2018/aug/17/simone-biles-gymnastics-olympics-interview.

2. Quoted in Susan Reed, "Arthur Ashe Remembers the Forgotten Men of Sport—America's Early Black Athletes," *People*, March 6, 1989. people.com/archive/arthur-ashe-remembers-the-forgotten-men-of-sport-americas-early-black-athletes-vol-31-no-9/.

3. Quoted in Peter Kelley, "Stories of Strength Shine in 'Better than the Best: Black Athletes Speak, 1920–2007,'" UW News, February 9, 2011. www.washington.edu/news/2011/02/09/stories-of-strength-shine-in-better-than-the-best-black-athletes-speak-1920-2007/.

Chapter One: Enslavement, Entertainment, and Escape

4. Quoted in William C. Rhoden, *Forty Million Dollar Slaves: The Rise, Fall, and Redemption of the Black Athlete*. New York, NY: Random House, 2006, p. 52.

5. L.A. Jennings, "Fighting the Shackles of Slavery: 'Kicking and Knocking' in the Antebellum South," Vice Sports, October 6, 2016. sports.vice.com/en_us/article/mgzb4v/fighting-the-shackles-of-slavery-kicking-and-knocking-in-the-antebellum-south.

6. Quoted in Russell T. Wigginton, *The Strange Career of the Black Athlete*. Westport, CT: Praeger, 2006, p. 6.

7. Quoted in Eli Capilouto, "Honoring Isaac Murphy, Learning from his Story," University of Kentucky News, October 9, 2018. uknow.uky.edu/blogs/president-capilou-to-s-blog/honoring-isaac-murphy-learning-his-story.

8. Quoted in Rhoden, *Forty Million Dollar Slaves*, p. 76.

9. Quoted in Lynne Tolman, "'Worcester Whirlwind' Overcame Bias," *Telegram & Gazette*, July 23, 1995. www.majortaylorassociation.org/whirlwind.htm.

10. Mark Conti, "Cycling: Statue Promotes Pioneer," Telegram.com, last updated June 17, 2010. www.

telegram.com/article/20100516/column31/5160571.

Chapter Two: New Century, Old Conflicts

11. Quoted in Rhoden, *Forty Million Dollar Slaves*, p. 81.

12. Mark Law, "Baseball Pioneer Honored," *Herald-Star*, October 8, 2018. www.heraldstaronline.com/news/local-news/2018/10/baseball-pioneer-honored/.

13. Quoted in Robert Peterson, *Only the Ball Was White: A History of Legendary Black Players and All Black Professional Teams*. New York, NY: Oxford University Press, 1970, p. 65.

14. Quoted in Peterson, *Only the Ball Was White*, p. 160.

15. Quoted in Larry Schwartz, "No Joshing About Gibson's Talents," ESPN, accessed on April 19, 2019. www.espn.com/sportscentury/features/00016050.html.

16. Quoted in M.B. Roberts, "Paige Never Looked Back," ESPN, accessed on April 23, 2019. www.espn.com/sportscentury/features/00016396.html.

17. Quoted in Roberts, "Paige Never Looked Back."

18. Quoted in "Unforgivable Blackness - About the Film," PBS, January 2005. www.pbs.org/weta/unforgivableblackness/about/.

19. Quoted in "Jack Johnson (1878-1946)," PBS, accessed on April 23, 2019. www.pbs.org/wgbh/americanexperience/features/fight-jack-johnson-1878-1946/.

20. Quoted in "Unforgivable Blackness - About the Film," PBS.

21. Quoted in Larry Schwartz, "'Brown Bomber' Was a Hero to All," ESPN, accessed on April 24, 2019. www.espn.com/sportscentury/features/00016109.html.

22. Quoted in Schwartz, "'Brown Bomber' Was a Hero to All."

23. Quoted in "Joe Louis (1914-1981)," PBS, accessed on April 24, 2019. www.pbs.org/wgbh/americanexperience/features/fight-joe-louis-1914-1981/.

24. Quoted in Larry Schwartz, "Owens Pierced a Myth," ESPN, accessed on April 24, 2019. www.espn.com/sportscentury/features/00016393.html.

25. Quoted in "About Jesse Owens," Jesse Owens Trust, accessed on April 24, 2019. www.jesseowens.com/about/.

Chapter Three: The Power of Protest

26. Quoted in Andrew Schall, "Wendell Smith: The Pittsburgh Journalist Who Made Jackie Robinson Mainstream," *Pittsburgh Post-Gazette*, June 5, 2011. www.

post-gazette.com/opinion/
Op-Ed/2011/06/05/The-Next-
Page-Wendell-Smith-The-
Pittsburgh-journalist-who-made-
Jackie-Robinson-mainstream/
stories/201106050161.

27. Quoted in David K. Wiggins, *Glory Bound: Black Athletes in a White America*. Syracuse, NY: Syracuse University Press, 1997, p. 91.

28. Quoted in Wiggins, *Glory Bound*, p. 101.

29. Quoted in Wiggins, *Glory Bound*, p. 102.

30. Quoted in Peterson, *Only the Ball Was White*, p. 190.

31. Quoted in Larry Schwartz, "Jackie Changed Face of Sports," ESPN, accessed on April 24, 2019. www.espn.com/sportscentury/features/00016431.html.

32. Quoted in Schwartz, "Jackie Changed Face of Sports."

33. John C. Walter, "The Changing Status of the Black Athlete in the 20th Century United States," *American Studies Today*, Summer 1996. www.americansc.org.uk/Online/walters.htm.

Chapter Four: With Rackets and Clubs

34. Quoted in Karen Crouse, "Treasure of Golf's Sad Past, Black Caddies Vanish in Era of Riches," *New York Times*, April 2, 2012. www.nytimes.com/2012/04/03/sports/golf/from-a-symbol-of-segregation-to-a-victim-of-golfs-success.html.

35. Quoted in Jim Gullo, "A Salute to Sweet Swinger," *Sports Illustrated*, May 31, 1993. www.si.com/vault/1993/05/31/128662/a-salute-to-sweet-swinger-jim-crow-rules-kept-teddy-sweet-swinger-rhodes-from-showing-the-world-his-great-talent.

36. Quoted in Gullo, "A Salute to Sweet Swinger."

37. Quoted in "PGA Historical Center Unveils African-American Pioneers Exhibit with Video Tributes to Ted Rhodes, John Shippen, Bill Spiller and Joe Louis," PGA of America, January 26, 2010. pdf.pgalinks.com/pgavillage/Jan_26_African_American_Pioneers.pdf.

38. Quoted in Steve Tignor, "American Tennis Association Changed the Face of Tennis in the U.S.," Tennis.com, December 5, 2016. www.tennis.com/pro-game/2016/12/american-tennis-association-changed-face-tennis-us/62274/.

39. Quoted in "Sport: That Gibson Girl," *TIME*, August 26, 1957. content.time.com/time/subscriber/article/0,33009,862710-2,00.html.

40. Quoted in Larry Schwartz, "Althea Gibson Broke Barriers," ESPN, accessed on April 26, 2019. www.espn.com/sportscentury/

features/00014035.html.

41. Quoted in Roxanne Jones and Jessie Paolucci, *Say It Loud: An Illustrated History of the Black Athlete*. New York, NY: Ballantine Books, 2010, p. 165.

42. Quoted in Schwartz, "Althea Gibson Broke Barriers."

43. Quoted in Jones and Paolucci, *Say It Loud*, p. 166.

44. Quoted in Bud Collins, "Arthur Ashe | Bio," ATP Tour, accessed on April 29, 2019. www.atptour.com/en/players/arthur-ashe/a063/bio.

Chapter Five: Using Their Voices

45. Quoted in George Vecsey, "Indomitable Russell Values One Accolade Above the Rest," *New York Times*, February 12, 2011. www.nytimes.com/2011/02/13/sports/basketball/13russell.html.

46. Quoted in Jones and Paolucci, *Say It Loud*, p. 76.

47. Quoted in Vecsey, "Indomitable Russell."

48. Quoted in Russell T. Wigginton, *The Strange Career of the Black Athlete*. Westport, CT: Praeger, 2006, p. 52.

49. Max Resetar, "BHM 2019: Bill Russell is a Basketall and Civil Rights Champion," Slam, February 8, 2019. www.slamonline.com/bhm2019/bhm-bill-russell/.

50. Quoted in Wigginton, *The Strange Career of the Black Athlete*, p. 57.

51. Quoted in Steve Rushin, "SI 60: 1954-94 How We Got Here Chapter 4: The Long, Hard Run," *Sports Illustrated*, August 5, 2014. www.si.com/more-sports/2014/08/05/si-60-how-we-got-here-jim-brown-steve-rushin-1994.

52. Quoted in Rushin, "SI 60."

53. Quoted in Wigginton, *The Strange Career of the Black Athlete*, p. 63.

54. Quoted in Jesse Abramson, "Cassius Clay Scores 'Incredible' Title Fight Triumph," *Ottawa Citizen*, February 28, 1964. news.google.com/newspapers?id=ZbMyAAAAIBAJ&sjid=i-wFAAAAIBAJ&pg=4391,2972708&dq=cassius+clay+defeats+liston&hl=en.

55. Quoted in Robert Lipsyte, "Clay Refuses Army Oath; Stripped of Boxing Crown," *New York Times*, April 29, 1967. archive.nytimes.com/www.nytimes.com/books/98/10/25/specials/ali-army.html.

56. Tia Mitchell, "The Louisville Lip: Muhammad Ali's Fighting Words Fueled a Movement," *Atlanta Journal-Constitution*, February 6, 2019. www.ajc.com/news/the-louisville-lip-muhammad-ali-fighting-words-fueled-movement/nplsvMU8pRfQJckG7uMjRM/.

57. Quoted in David Davis, "Olympic Athletes Who Took a Stand,"

Smithsonian, August 2008. www. smithsonianmag.com/articles/ olympic-athletes-who-took-a-stand-593920/.

58. Quoted in Amy Bass, *Not the Triumph but the Struggle: The 1968 Olympics and the Making of the Black Athlete*. Minneapolis, MN: University of Minnesota Press, 2002, p. 271.

59. Quoted in Kevin G. Andrade, "Olympic Medalist, Civil-Rights Icon John Carlos Urges Audience at URI to Do their Part," *Providence Journal*, February 13, 2019. www.providencejournal. com/news/20190213/olympic-medalist-civil-rights-icon-john-carlos-urges-audience-at-uri-to-do-their-part--audio.

60. Quoted in Steve Wyche, "Colin Kaepernick Explains Why He Sat During National Anthem," NFL.com, last updated August 28, 2016. www.nfl.com/news/ story/0ap3000000691077/ article/colin-kaepernick-explains-why-he-sat-during-national-anthem.

Chapter Six: Making History, Changing Minds

61. Jacob Poore, "Why Tiger Woods Is One of the Greatest Athletes Ever," *Odyssey*, May 17, 2016. www. theodysseyonline.com/why-tiger-woods-is-the-goat.

62. Quoted in Jason La Canfora, "NFL's 'QB Summit' to Be the Next Step in Addressing Lack of Diversity in Coaching," CBS Sports, February 3, 2019. www.cbssports.com/nfl/ news/nfls-qb-summit-to-be-the-next-step-in-addressing-lack-of-diversity-in-coaching/.

63. Quoted in La Canfora, "NFL's 'QB Summit' to Be the Next Step."

FOR MORE INFORMATION

Books

Biles, Simone. *Courage to Soar: A Body in Motion, A Life in Balance*. Grand Rapids, MI: Zondervan Books, 2016.
This memoir by Biles focuses on how she prepared for a life in gymnastics.

Burgan, Michael. *Olympic Gold 1936: How the Image of Jesse Owens Crushed Hitler's Evil Myth*. North Mankato, MN: Compass Point Books, 2017.
Learn about how Jesse Owens won the 1936 Olympics and shocked the world.

Roberts, Russell. *Breaking the Barriers (Swinging for the Fences: Life in the Negro Leagues)*. Kennett Square, PA: Purple Toad Publishing, 2017.
This book is part of a series that explores the time period when baseball was still segregated.

Smith-Llera, Danielle. *Black Power Salute: How a Photograph Captured a Political Protest*. North Mankato, MN: Compass Point Books, 2017.
This book focuses on the moment when Tommie Smith and John Carlos won Olympic medals in 1968 and made a silent protest against racial injustice.

Zuckerman, Gregory. *Rising Above: Inspiring Women in Sports*. London, England: Puffin Books, 2019.
Learn about 10 female athletes, including Wilma Rudolph, Mo'ne Davis, Venus and Serena Williams, and Simone Biles.

Websites

Fun Facts about Black American Athletes
www.fun-facts.org.uk/black-americans/black-american-athletes.htm
This website offers facts and trivia about numerous black athletes, including Serena Williams and LeBron James.

HISTORY: Jim Crow Laws
www.history.com/topics/early-20th-century-us/jim-crow-laws
Read about the history of African Americans' struggle for their basic civil rights on this website.

Kid World Citizen: Black History - Biographies for Kids
kidworldcitizen.org/black-history-biographies-kids/
A list of biographies of famous African Americans is included here.

National Baseball Hall of Fame
baseballhall.org
This website features biographies, career statistics, and a transcript of the induction speech for each member of the Baseball Hall of Fame.

Negro Leagues Baseball Museum
nlbm.com
Learn about the history of the Negro leagues on this website. There is also a link to an e-museum with player and team profiles.

PBS: African-American Athletes
www.pbs.org/opb/historydetectives/feature/african-american-athletes/
The PBS website links to its History Detectives series, which includes biographies and documentaries about African American athletes throughout history.

INDEX

PICTURE CREDITS

ABOUT THE AUTHOR

Tamra Orr is the author of more than 500 nonfiction/educational books for readers of all ages. She graduated from Ball State University in Muncie, Indiana, with a degree in English and Education. She planned on becoming an English teacher. Instead, she moved to Oregon and began writing books. She has been fascinated by all elements of history for years and appreciates the chance to explore and discover more about different time periods and important figures.